REDNECK:
By a South Georgia Redneck

You May Not Like This Book!

A Book of Stories by

Sammie L. O'Steen

REDNECK:
By a South Georgia Redneck
You May Not Like This Book
Sammie L. O'Steen

This book may not be reproduced in whole or part, in any manner whatsoever, without written permission, with the exception of brief quotations within book reviews or articles.

Published December 2023
Indy Pub
Copyright © 2023 Sammie L. O'Steen
All rights reserved
ISBN: 979-8-8690-2983-6 (Paperback)
ISBN: 979-8-8690-2984-3 (E-Book)

Introduction

Yeah, I've been thinking about this a long time. In fact, I started it one time before and quit. I'd probably quit again if it had not been for meeting Sal. Had I not run into him, I would have never finished.

This is just a mixture of things that I've had happened in my life, people that I know, and the things that have happened in their lives. They're all comical. I've talked to a lot of people and told these stories over and over. They have me tell them again, so some people must like them.

I never intended to write a book; I have had anxiety problems. I would ride my golf cart with my little puppy dog, and I would think of all these stories. It seemed to help my situation. I have been doing this for fourteen years. But this book is for a certain type of people. If you don't like to bull-shoot, if you don't like to fish, if you're not a redneck, if you don't like a little alcohol, then, you're probably not going to enjoy this book. You'll just have to make up your own mind about that. Some of these stories are a little bit smutty, and I can't help that.

I was expected to finish high school and college, go to work, get married, have kids and live a happy life, which is not the way it worked. I married three- and one-half times. The last half is not over yet. I married her twice. I am not proud of myself. I broke a lot of hearts. I don't know what happened.

Between one of those times, I ran into SNEAKIE SNAKE. That was a big mistake. We were crying in our beer over some of the same problems and we bonded quickly. We went on to do some of these crazy things. The rest were done by people I know. ALL TRUE. Some of them I would like to do over and others I am glad I don't have to. This book is just a good sample. I am going to try to keep your attention by scattering some of the best ones throughout the book. One being SNEAKIE, and you will see how Sneakie he really was. Another one is, MUTT and JEFF who were brothers and part time drunks. They always wanted an old boat and motor but couldn't get them at the same time. They had to buy beer, which was more important. EL TIGHTO, didn't drink but he was a good businessman. If you did not watch him, he will steal your britches. BATMAN—insurance salesman. I think he got caught stealing company money, left town and never returned. My COUSIN—he would get drunk and do crazy things. Also, CROWBAR—I am going to let you wonder about him.

Crowbar

We graduated from the high school and some of us decided to go to Atlanta to make our fortunes. One of the young men was named Crowbar. We named him that because we thought he was dumb. He and I were riding around on a Saturday night on the express way. He had an old car that would shake and pull to one side once in a while. An old Buick pulled up beside us and it shook towards him. Crowbar straightened it up and we carried on. In a few minutes the Buick pull back up beside us and it shook towards him again. He was with his girlfriend. He shouted to us, "Pull over and I'll whip your ass." Crowbar said, "Let's pull over and whip his ass." I told him to just slow down and let him go on. He replied with, "Hell no."

We got off at the next exit and he followed us. I will never forget it was a dead-end road with a cul-de-sac. And there was a pile of trash and a night light at the end. Crowbar stopped and jumped out and I stayed in the car. I was not in a hurry. The other man jumped out and his girlfriend started racing the motor. I don't think that was the first time they had done this. He got about ten feet from Crowbar and he had a blackjack with a long handle. He yelled, "HII-YAA-KAII-YAA," and hit Crowbar in the head. He kept on talking crazy names and hitting Crowbar at the same time. Crowbar went down and he kept hitting him. I knew I had to help him, so I ran towards the man and he started chasing me. I started running around the trash pile and he was still yelling, "HII-YAA-KAII-

YAA." Crowbar had made it to the car and locked the doors. The man was chasing me round and round the car but he could not catch me, so he started knocking Crowbar's window out so he could hit him in the head some more. Crowbar finally unlocked the door and let me in. We got back on the express way and looked for a hospital sign. Finally spotted one and I took him inside. Crowbar had a banlon shirt on. He pulled it off and blood poured all over the floor. They had to shave his head but he did not have to have stitches. He said, "The next Saturday night we were going to get him. I replied, "You may be, but I ain't going."

Mr. Fred

One morning, I was off to a bad start. I got up to go to the coffee shop and my battery was dead. I'd left my truck switched on. If you go by signs, that ain't a good sign. So that means I might not have a good day today, or maybe I'm wrong. I hoped so anyhow.

This guy from my hometown loved to fish and loved to go down to the coast. There's a place down there where the government keeps our submarines—they won't admit you to go all the way to base—they've got two signs, one on the west end and one on the east end, and as long as you stay to the other side of those signs, they won't bother you. You just kind of have to eyeball it and stay inside those signs. Well, you know how people are; they always fudge. This particular time was right after the World Trade Center bombing and it wasn't a good time to be fudging. I'm surprised they even let you go in there to start with. There were two boats fudging and it wasn't long before the DNR or whatever you call them come out there and told them to get back on the other side and they said, "Yes, sir. "By the way, do either one of you have a camera?"

They said, "No, sir, we don't have a camera."

"Well, we need to check your belongings and see what you've got." Unbeknownst to the guy that owned the boat, the other guy had one of them little $5.00 cameras you get at Wal-Mart, just to take a picture of a fish or whatever if they come across something while they were fishing. I've got one myself. They spotted that camera and they took those guys right on up to the base. And it's funny, this guy telling this story is real comical like. I can't tell it like he did, but they got them to the base and they stood with their hands on their head for six hours. They were questioning them like were they terrorists. He was scared that they were going to go to jail. Towards the last, they found out this fellow was an idiot. I like him.

The other fellow in the other boat said, "Well, I'm going to tell y'all what. I'm leaving. We haven't done anything wrong but go fishing and y'all can't hold us."

The DNR man said, "No, sir, we can't hold you. You can go any time you want to. But you see that PT boat out there with that submachine gun on it? When you get about 30 yards away, we can cut that thing half because you're trespassing."

The guy said, "Well, I think I'll just wait until y'all get through." He knew he didn't want none of that. Oh, and they had even checked their sandwiches. They took them apart and checked in between the mayonnaise and the bologna to see if there was a bomb in there. And they had them slip corks you use down there in saltwater fishing into a plastic thing. They tore them apart and looked inside of them to be sure they didn't have a bomb in there. They checked them thoroughly. They found out he was a good guy; he just wasn't really smart. Right before they left, the guy told them in his real country talking accent, "You are smarter than me...I did not go to school. I had to go to work and I know you all went to college. All I did was work, fish and hunt, but I tell you what, I am smarter than y'all."

They replied, "Why do you say that Mr. Fred?"

"If y'all keep bringing people up here like this, one day you will have one person who has a real bomb and he will blow the hell out of all of you."

Dumbo 3 Dorman

This story is about a guy in my hometown who got work done by a lot of people. His wife wanted some work done at the house, so he had a Mexican who was a real good worker. He took him to his house and told him, "Now, you do anything she tells you to do." He left and stayed gone about two hours. His wife called him and said, "Come get this guy!"

He said, "What?"

She said, "Come get him to work."

"He won't work?"

She said, "No, he's sitting down over there like he's pouting."

"Well, my Lord. I'll come over there and see what's wrong."

He went home and asked him "Joe, what's wrong with you?"

Joe said, "Me no work for woman."

He said, "What?"

Joe said, "Me no work for woman." He had to carry him back to the shop; he wouldn't work for the woman!

Food Stamps

I went down to the carwash one day and the guys working there didn't see me, but I could hear what they were talking about around the corner. They were talking about food stamps. None of them think they were getting enough food stamps. "They ought to give them more." Another guy said, "Well, they sure ain't giving me enough." He said, "I don't get but $350 a month worth of food stamps and my wife just had another baby. I feel like they need to give me a raise." I think you can be too good to people.

Dumbo Colonoscopy

I don't know if ya'll are familiar with a colonoscopy, that checks you for cancer of your colon or something or another, but you're probably familiar. If you're on up in there in age, like I am, you've probably had one. Well, let me give you some good advice: don't ever eat any chocolate pie before you have a colonoscopy.

They had me signed up to have mine at three o'clock that next afternoon. Well, my Lord, you've fasted all the way from nine o'clock the night before and all day the next day. I called and tried to get them to change it to where I could have it in the morning, I chew tobacco and I like to eat. I remember one time before I had mine in the morning, but no, they couldn't do that. Right at the very last minute before I was supposed to go at three o'clock, it hit me. There was one little piece of chocolate pie in the icebox, and it was just worrying the devil out of me. I said, "Well, being this is going to be so close I can probably eat this piece of chocolate pie and get by with it because it won't have time to digest and go down in my colon." So I ate the piece of chocolate pie. I went and had my colonoscopy and they called me back and they said, "Dumbo, it didn't show up. It was cloudy." I didn't say nothing about the chocolate pie. I didn't know whether that had anything to do with it or not. "You need to go over to the hospital and let them run another kind of test on you."

"Well, okay."

So, I went over there, and they went to undressing me and putting a gown on me. I said, "What the hell is going on?" They said, "Well, we're going to have to do..."

I said, "Wait a minute now, this ain't what I signed up for now." And I showed myself out. They finally had to call my wife and she came down there.

And then the doctor called me. Well, what it amounted to...I don't know a pretty way to say it, and I ain't trying to be ugly...BUT they inserted a thing in my—I reckon rectum is about as good a word as I can think of—in my rectum and they hung a bag up there full of some kind of white, looked like milk or something in a jug, and they put me on a machine and you know—how they do a woman when she's having a baby. They put my arms in something, and they spread my legs and kind of put me in stirrups. I was laying there spread eagle. And that damn machine, it was like a Ferris Wheel. That thing just spun me around and around and back this a-way and then that-a-way and the other way and all the time it was doing that, the white mess was running in my eyes and all over my legs and my belly. I had on just a little gown—where your tail and everything is showing. That lasted, I guess, 20 minutes. I got out of that thing and I had to go take a shower, because that mess was all over me. I felt like I'd been cleaned out. They did another test on me after that and said that I was now good and clean inside. Well, I kind of figured that. But the only thing I want is to give you is some good advice—do not eat any chocolate pie before you have a colonoscopy.

James Brown

I had a guy in my hometown—he and his two brothers who had a little construction business and they were very successful. After about 20 years, one of the brothers had a mini stroke. It didn't affect him to look at him, but somehow it affected his mind a little bit, and he would just get mad and just go into fits. This began to cause problems with the company. They had a big company that did high-end work on buildings. The help got scared of him and the people in the office, too. One of his foreman came in the office and they got into a fight. When they did, they saw that they had to remove him somehow. Everything they'd ever done, they did together. The brothers were that close. They had a good bit of property and the only way they could do it was to divide it. They treated the brother who had the stroke terribly bad. He was depressed, and I think he had thoughts of killing himself. He just couldn't believe that his brother would do him like that. Not long after that, he found out that he had prostate cancer. The doctor told him that it was curable. But this guy was kind of a Rambo. He was short and stocky and tough. He had always been that way. Just a tough guy. He was in such a state of mind over his situation that he told the doctor, "I don't want to treat it. I'm ready to die." I know he regretted that many times. I know I would have. He didn't get it treated. He lived a year to a year and a half.

He and I, we'd go to the restaurant and eat breakfast every morning, and we watched the football games together. He's got a horse barn he converted into a bull shooting shack. He had an old wood heater in there and had old antiques, and he had skinned out snakes and raccoons. They had a place up at the river for 50 years, and he really liked to go there, drink a little beer and just have a good time. When he had this mini stroke, he'd come in the restaurant once in a while and he'd get mad with somebody, and just go berserk, and want to fight.

This one particular time he came, and I don't remember what it was over, he jumped on me, and went to snatching his coat off, and by that time he'd gotten to where he couldn't hardly walk and couldn't get up and down, they'd calmed him down. It embarrassed him. He didn't come back for about a week or two. I didn't think much about it because I knew he'd done it to several people before then.

Once they were there cooking breakfast over there, and he cracked one of the eggs and it didn't do right. He had a full flat of those eggs and he just took them one at a time and threw them and busted them on the wall. Just that kind of stuff. He just couldn't control his short temper.

After what happened to me, he called me to his house about a week later and apologized to me. "Now, if you want me to, I'll get on my hands and knees and apologize to you" he said. "But you'll have to help me up, but I'll sure get down there and do it."

And this fellow gave a good amount of money to the church. He said, "Preacher, I can't catch up. I've been a sinner all my life and I may go to hell, but I'm fixing to try to change." He just had a different frame of mind and he got religion.

Two or three days before Christmas he called me over to his house. "I've got something for you." He had me a rod and a reel. I mean a high-priced rod and a reel.

"Man, you don't have to do that," I said.

He said, "Oh, I want to. I'm so ashamed of the way I did you. And I'll get on my hands and knees right now again if you want me to."

"No—no, don't worry about it."

He weighed about 300 pounds and he could walk some, but he couldn't get up and down. He had some medicine and I asked him, "Do you want me to go get the medicine for you?"

He said, "No, I don't need it right now." And this guy walked in. I'm glad he showed up. He had dropped the medicine and was on the floor trying to get it and he couldn't get up. I couldn't have gotten him up by myself. But at that time, he was alert and could talk. I won't say he was doing good, but at least he acted normal. He died the next day. He said that he had done a lot of people wrong and was trying to right his wrongs before he died. Everybody that he could think of that he had done wrong, he wanted to get hold of them and straighten it out. I really appreciate what he did for me. He got me a rod and reel. I hope he is in peace.

Wrong Woman

I took my wife to the Red Lobster and ate and had a wonderful time and we bonded a little bit. She just had to go to Belk's...you know how women are. We got ready to leave, and I come out ahead of her and went to the car. I opened the car door and a woman said, "You're getting in the wrong car."

I said, "What?"

It wasn't my wife, it was another woman. I said, "I'm sorry."

She said, "Don't worry about it. My husband done the same thing."

Ring

I was working out at the beach one time, and me and a guy that worked there got off work, parked on the back of the Jax Liquor parking lot and drank beer. We were there one night drinking beer and this brand-new Cadillac come wheeling through there and pulled up beside us. The guy looked all around like he was scared. He said, "Y'all want to buy a ring?"

It just so happened my buddy had a ring; some kind of Masonic ring or something that he said was a real nice diamond, and he liked rings. "Y'all want to buy a ring?" the guy asked again.

We were drinking, and boy, he jumped right on it. "What kind of ring you got?" And this guy come out with a ring that was a cluster. It was as big around as a quarter, them clusters of diamonds. It was in the original box and all just like in the jewelry store. It had a price on it, four or $5,000.

My buddy said, "No, we can't buy that."

He said, "Well, I'll sell it cheap."

And my buddy said, "What do you call cheap?"

He said, "$500." That kind of got our attention So we kept on a-jawing and kept on talking and finally I bought the ring. I talked him into letting me buy it because he already had one. I bought it for a hundred dollars. Boy, I went to work the next day and had that thing on. There was this guy in there that liked jewelry, and I showed it to him. He offered me a thousand dollars for it right then. I could have made some money, but I didn't have that much sense. I was after the whole nut. So, I wore that thing for about a week or two, and I figured it was hot. So, I decided to find out what it was really worth. I tried to think up a lie to tell at the jewelry store. I finally told them I found on the beach. I showed it to the man at the jewelry store. He didn't even put that eye thing on. Sometimes I think that's the joke. I said, "How much is this ring worth?"

He said, "It's at least worth $7." Ain't that the pits?

That night, we rode around all over the beach, drinking. Every time we'd go in the bathroom, we'd scratch it on the mirrors. Boy, it would cut just like a diamond, so I thought I had really captured the moon. Guess not.

Dumbo—Trailer Park

I bought an old mobile home park in a bad section of town, but it was kind of unique. It was off the road up in the woods. It was pretty up to and scenic. It had big oak trees and pine trees and several trailers in there in good condition, and it looked good to me. I got a good price on it. After I bought it, somebody asked me, "You know who you got out there, don't you?"

I said, "No."

There wasn't but one of them rented. That seemed a little strange to me when just one of them was rented because it looked like a good place. He told me who he was, and I knew him. He was a drunk.

He told me that the whole bunch comes out there and drinks and parties every day. There ain't nobody around to run them off and they can just do like they want too. That's just a party house. Sure enough, I went out there the next night to see and there must have been 15 or 20 automobiles pulled up there in the yard.

Uh-huh, I could see now why nobody is renting these trailers. All these drunks are keeping them run off. Now, they were rough. So, the next day I went to see him, "Listen, you're going to have to move," I said. "You can't stay here. This is what's keeping my trailers from renting and I've got too much money tied up in this thing, so you're going to have to move. I'll give you two weeks to get out of here."

Well, he didn't say nothing, but I could tell he didn't like it. The next day I was working on one of the old trailers and a guy came to over to me, one of his drinking buddies, and told me that he was mad. He told me about one of his buddies that was mad, and he was a big and rough. Sure enough, it was the one with them big ol' fists. I couldn't stand them ol' big fists. He told me he was going to come over there and really work on me. That thing scared me because I wasn't able to fight 'nare one of them, and there might have more than one come.

So, I went home and got my gun and came back. I tried to work on the trailer and look out the doors and windows and be sure they weren't coming. I was scared to do anything. I didn't know what to do.

It just so happened I was working over at a man's mobile home park, and he was remodeling old mobile homes, buying them and putting them in there. I asked him," Do you want to buy a mobile home?"

He said, "Well, what have you got?"

I told him, and I gave him a cheap price. He said, "Well, let's go look at it."

It wasn't far, so we rode around the corner and looked at it. "And you'll take that much for it?" he asked.

I said, "I'd take that for it. But one thing though...it's got to be moved."

He said, "Okay, it'll have to be moved. Let me go in and look at it."

I said, " I ain't going up there. You can go up there, but I ain't going up there. I was scared of them like they were a damn rattlesnake. He walked up to the door and they opened it and evidently, they knew him. He was retired from the Merchant Marines.

"Hey Vernon! How you doing?"

"Fine. I've been fine."

There were eight or ten of them up there drinking and carrying on. He looked at them and said, "I've come to look at this trailer. I might be going to buy it. Do you mind if I come in and look at it?"

He said, "Oh, no, no, just come right on in. Just look all you want to, Vernon. Yeah, just any way you can."

Vernon went in and looked around and come back in a few minutes and said, "You said you'd take that much for it?"

I said, "Yeah."

He counted out the money to me, and he said, "You just sold it."

"Now, wait a minute. It's got to be moved."

He said, "It'll be moved as quickly as possible."

He walked back up to the door and they were all standing up there peeping out the windows and looking out the door. He told the man—his name was Sam—"Sam, I've just bought this trailer. Now, you've got three choices. I've got another trailer over there already finished that you can move in right now. You can start moving your stuff out of there and put it in mine. Or you can stay in this trailer and when I get ready to move it you can just stay in it and I'll move you, furniture and everything at one time. Or if you don't want to do one of those two things, get your stuff out of here right now."

He said, "Yes, sir, Vernon. I'll tell you what I'll do. Yeah, I'll just take that other trailer you've got. I'll just move right on over there. That will be fine."

Oh, and another thing he told him, "I'm going to tell you right now, we're not going to have the kind of partying over there that you're doing here. If you do, I'm going to run you off in a hurry."

"No, Vernon. No, we'll be fine. We won't have no trouble," Sam said. He stayed five to seven years with him, and as far as I know he stayed there until he died. But I just couldn't handle them kind of people.

Dumbo Fishing

Yeah, when I started this thing—I started this one time before and I quit with it, and I've started it again and seems like it's just a good mind for me. I'm kind of enjoying talking about things. But all this is a lot of war stories. It's past stories of things that I have done. It's mainly screw-ups.

My name, the fish bait man named me, Dumbo. That's Dumbo. The reason being, I have screwed up so many times, nearly drowned several times, with my fishing. One of the times, I went up to the river by myself, and backed my boat in the water and didn't have the rope tied. It floated off. To make a long story short, there was a hole I didn't know they had dug at the bottom of the landing. I dropped off in the hole and went under and got back up and swam out and caught the boat. The wind was blowing it away. And I don't know if you're familiar with boats, but on the back-hand corner, if the same thing happened to you—don't ever—and you need to write this down somewhere—don't ever grab for the corners, either the right-hand or left-hand corner at the back of the boat. Don't ever grab for there because in most of your boats there's a flat piece welded on the top on those back corners. I suppose to give it support. I lunged over and grabbed at the back of that boat and my hand hit that slick part and I slid down and I went under. I came back up and the boat had moved some more. I paddled on out and lunged again and the same thing. And I said to myself, "You're going to drown right here."

The thing is, it wasn't 50-foot wide, and except for that hole, none of it was over three or four-foot deep. It was in the summertime, and it was real shallow. Common sense would have told you all I had to do was stand up, probably when I got out of that hole, and was in no danger, but when you panic you don't think about that. So, I went under that second time and I said, "You're fixin' to drown right here." I lunged that last time. I went further over the boat that time, and I caught the steering cable on the boat. Then, I dog paddled over to the other side. I was still in the water trying to catch my breath and somebody came up and said, "You need some help?"

I said, "I've got it now."

The next time they went in the bait house they told the bait man all about it, and he told everybody else. I had to hear that for two or three months. The fish bait man refuses to sell me any bait if I don't have somebody with me. He claims that he's not going to be responsible for me drowning.

So, I'll go fishing. In my age bracket, they're all dying out, or don't care nothing about fishing, or their wives won't let them go. I'll wind up going myself, but if I'm going to go, I have to take somebody with me, even if they're not going. I have to pick me up somebody and take them to the fish bait house, because, if I don't, he won't sell me no bait. That ain't right, is it? That's discrimination.

Batman & the Go-Go Girls

We were playing poker one night. By the way, there's two or three things a young person don't need to do. I'm older and wiser, and I've been there and done all a lot. It's caused me a lot of heart break and I can tell you from experience: don't gamble, don't drink and, of course, sure don't do drugs. I never did drugs, but probably would have tried if I had been in that era. I hope I'd been one of the lucky ones who didn't catch it. It don't catch all of them, but I'd have tried it and I hate to say it, but it's the truth. Now, on with the story.

We were playing poker one night. We had a regular poker game and I was addicted to it, and it cost me a family. About nine o'clock, my buddy—I say he was my buddy, but he was just an acquaintance—we were playing poker. They called him Batman. I never have figured out why, but that's what they called him. And he was a good winner and I was winning a little, not nearly as much as he was. They had just started with that topless dancing. When it very first came out, we'd never seen that and we decided to just quit playing poker while we were winning and go see the go-go's…the topless go-go's. We took off down there and it was just like they said it was. It was topless go-go's. I enjoyed it for a while, but after you watch it a while it gets old. I started playing pool. I'd come up once in a while to get a beer and look over at Batman and this other guy with us. He didn't have any money. He was just going along for a free ride with Batman and, boy, he was spending it freely.

I looked over there the first time I came in, and he had one bra on his head. When I come over there the third time, he had two or three bras on his head. Well, that should have told me something right then, but I didn't have sense enough to realize it. I don't know what time it was, but we closed that place down that night. He had an old car which was an old Chevrolet. We'd been real smart and filled it up with gas when we got there first thing, so we didn't have to worry about running out of gas.

We left and went down to the Krystal. I think that was all that was open at that time of the night. We were going to eat us some chili and Batman says, "Dumbo, you got any money?"

I said, "Hell no, I ain't got any money."

And he said, "Well hell, I ain't either. I spent it all."

"You mean you spent all that money?" I asked.

He said, "Hell, yeah! I spent every penny of it."

I said, "Man, you're crazy."

Well, the other man didn't have any money and I didn't have but $2.00 or $3.00 or something like that. All we were going to do was turn around and go back home. So that wound up that party up.

We started back home and I didn't know his car used transmission fluid. It used transmission fluid about the same way that a lot of these cars use gas. We got about half-way back and started up one of them hills. We were down in Florida. Whenever you come up them hills, when coming back, well, it's hillier. We got to going up them hills and that damn transmission went to spinning, and it got worse and worse. When we topped the last hill coming in, I was so glad to see my county and the city limits. It was about three, four, five o'clock in the morning, and by then we were all dead. But at that last hill, there's a big creek there, so, there's a high hill to climb. That motor was going wide open, and I bet you it wasn't going but three miles an hour, but bless its heart, it made it all the way up the hill and we came home. That's just another one of my episodes.

Batman Years Later

I was working in this town, and run across Batman in a bar. He said that he had a new job but did not have anywhere to stay, so I let him stay with me. During the week, I agreed to let his girlfriend stay until the payday. Then, he was going to pay me some rent and for all the beer he and his girlfriend drank at the bar. So, every morning I would get up early and before I get to work which was about 5:00 a.m. and take him to his job first and take his girlfriend somewhere downtown. It was a big company he was working for and behind the security fence with guards. It looked like he had a pretty good job. Now, that payday, I went to pick him up and we were going to get drink. He was going to pay me what he owed. I got there a few minutes early because you can't trust everybody, especially Batman. So, I waited and waited…no Batman. I finally went up to security guard and asked him if he was working late? He told me no, and he would check his roster.

"Sir, I don't see his name, so he is not working late."

I said, "He works here because I have been bringing him to work every morning."

He said, "Let me check my roster again. No sir, nobody with that name works here."

I said, "Well…that lying SOB. He's been staying with me, and I have been paying for his beer and spending money on him and his girlfriend and bringing him to work early every morning…and that SOB doesn't even work there!"

That's the reason I do not have friends. I have associates.

Years later, I was down in the town and I just rode down main street near where the bus pulls up at the park. There's always a lot of people and most of them bums. I just happened to glance around the park bench and I spotted him immediately. It was Batman. I pulled over in the bus lane just to be sure. Thanks goodness he did not see me. He had one of his legs propped, and it looked like he had paper in the bottom of his shoes for soles. His hair was long, dirty nasty, and he had a raggedy beard. That was the last time I saw him. I feel like he died a drunk bum.

Lost Things

You never quit learning, I don't think. Still, as old as I am, I learn things every day. I learned something last night that I should have discovered a long time ago. I have trouble. If you've got any age on you and you're reading this thing, you can relate to it, but I have trouble losing things. I can sit in one place and lose everything. It's just like that all day long. If I drop something on the floor, I just watch it, and I'll guarantee you it's going to wind up under the table or under the couch where I'm not going to be able to find it.

I've got a son, and I tickle the devil out of him. I watch for breaks, just like I'm going through a red light hoping it's green. If I get more traffic lights on green, it makes me feel like I'm going to have a better day. But if I hit them all red, I'll say, "Well, this is going to be a hell of a day."

I was down at my son's house and we were having lettuce, tomato and mayonnaise sandwiches. I smeared some mayonnaise on my bread and the next thing I did is somehow knocked it off on the floor. I told my son, "Well, I'll be dogged. I've got a break."

He asked, "What do you mean?"

I said, "Hell, it didn't go down on the mayonnaise side."

Boy, that thing tickled him. I picked it up, finished making my sandwich and ate it.

But one of the things that I learned, and I don't know why it's taken me so long, but I found out I have trouble when I fix me cereal every night. I mean I enjoy my cereal. I've been trying to lose weight for 40 years. They've got these mixed fruits in these bags that's frozen, and I take it, and the first thing I do is I go ahead and take out the mixed fruit and put it where it can be thawing out. Then I start getting my other ingredients. I've found out that I'm more like my daddy every day. He does about the same routine. And then, I'll have to buy me a peach and I'll have to slice it up in it. Then I have to mix about half cereal and about half raisin bran. It just takes longer that way, but that's just the way I like it. I sit down, and I've forgot my juice. I drink me a glass of that cranberry juice every night. That AARP thing says that it's real good for you for several things. Well, I'll be forgot that. I've got to get up, and when you do that, your cereal is getting soggy. I've tried to figure every way in the world to speed this thing up where my cereal wouldn't be soggy, but I ain't really got it figured out yet.

The damn dogs will want to go out or come in—they're always something. The telephone will ring or there's some sort of an inconvenience when you're doing something that you enjoy. What I learned is that with my cereal and my spoon—and I realize I forget my napkins now. You've got to have your napkins. I usually have to get up and get them. But I've found out one thing...if I'll go ahead and put my spoon in my cereal, I won't have to get another one. I can sit down with my cereal and when I sit down, I'll won't have to say, "Well, I'll be dogged, I didn't get my spoon." But if I forget, I've got to get my spoon, when I get up, and then, I find out that I've got it in my lap, and of course, then I've knocked it off on the floor. When I do, I just pick it up and sit back down and eat with it. But the best way is to go ahead and put your spoon in your cereal to start with and that will save you a trip.

And the other thing I learned, and this is going to sound a little bit ugly and I don't know a real clean way to say it, but my bathroom habits are not regular, and when I go, I go. And I feel swelled or something, but this morning I got up and I could tell I needed to tend to that. So, it hit me, I said. "I'm going to weigh before I go to the bathroom." I weighed;

it was 189 pounds. I went and tended to business and went back in there and weighed and I had lost four pounds. That's just something I've been intending to do for several years. I lost four pounds right quick.

Lost Keys

There was one time I was out at the club and this guy came in, and he'd lost his keys and couldn't get in the car. He wound up having to call the law to come out there and open his door for him. When they got out there, both of his back doors were unlocked. They saw he was drunk, and they just loaded him up and carried him to jail.

Free Food and Lunch

Well, I just had another brilliant idea. I just come out of the grocery store. I run in there to grab me a thing of ice cream. I've been wanting some walnut ice cream and it's hard to find anymore. Believe it or not, a guy come walking by there, and this was at Harvey's, I want to be sure and tell that. I had looked all up and down that ice cream aisle. I didn't know they made so many kinds of ice cream. There's rocky road, and the fudge kind, and the pineapple kind, and this kind, and that kind, and every kind but walnut, and there wasn't no walnut up there. I just asked him as a last chance, I said, "Y'all got any walnut ice cream?"

I thought maybe I might have just overlooked it. He pulled some of the ice cream out of the front and reached in the back, and finally found me a thing of walnut ice cream I certainly appreciated that he did that.

I got up to the counter to pay and naturally there was two people with full buggies in front of me, and they had one line open. I can't brag on that too much. I noticed when they went to pay, they both pulled out 'them' cards. I think they call them peach cards. And on top of that, both of them didn't have enough money on their cards. The one in the front went in her pocket and come out with some money, and that wasn't enough. She had to go in another pocket, and that wasn't quite enough either. She then had to do something else, and then finally they got through with hers. The next one was about the same way, only she had some of her money in her bra. I think we just ought to go ahead and give everybody free groceries, and then we wouldn't have to worry about that, and there wouldn't be no more standing in lines.

I heard this morning, something like 75-percent of the school children get free lunches. There's some people that pay for their lunch that really don't have the money. It's just that they've got the pride and they don't want the free lunch. It's like me. I've got a little pride, I guess, and the only way I would let my children have free lunches would be cause I just didn't have the money. There's a lot of people like me, I hope, that don't want a free ride. It appears to me we'd be better off just to give everybody a free lunch and be done with it.

Christmas Trees

I had a friend who lived not too far from me. He had a horse and he kept him in the backyard. I'd go over there and spend the night with my friend. He had a little shack outback that they'd fixed up for the him, and we'd spend the night in that shack. Well, the golf club wasn't too far away from his house.

It was two or three weeks until Christmas, and we came up with an idea. All around that golf club there was Christmas trees planted. We took that horse and went and climbed over the fence at the golf club. This was like late at night and he cut them off and I'd drag them and tie them to the horse and then we would drag them to his house and hide them until the next day. I think we was out for the holidays. We started selling them. We'd drag them around on that damn horse and sell them. We sold every one of them. Boys, we were like that it was big money to us. So, we decided the next time to go get the mother load.

We had to be over 16 years old. The next time we took my daddy's car, and instead of going on a horse in the middle of the night, we went late one evening and backed up to the fence and went to cutting us a load. Suddenly, there was three or four cars coming from different angles, blocking us in, and we took off.

There was a dam there, and we took off around the dam. We were going to get away from them, but they had the dam blocked off, so they stopped us and scared us to death. They told us if we would get a little job and pay for the Christmas trees, they wouldn't tell our mamas and daddies. So, we agreed to that. Well, guess what? The next Friday night or Saturday night we took that damn horse and went back out there in the middle of the night and did the same thing. He'd jumped the fence and get the trees, and I'd tie them up to the horse and we drug them out. We got just enough to pay our fine, cause we took them to town and sold them the next day, and paid them for the Christmas trees. That wound that up and we never did that again.

William Train

This other associate of mine I mentioned a while ago, the one that said his wife was so tough that if they broke in, they'd break out, liked to buy cheap stuff. He wouldn't buy anything good. I've always been just the opposite.

He bought cheap stuff and then tried to make something out of it. He bought a house by the railroad tracks. That was the first thing against it. Most people don't want to live by a railroad track. And the other bad thing about it was it was across the street from these apartments and it was low-end rent and there was about 40 or 50 of them. I'm sure he got a good, cheap price on it. I never did ask him. But he stayed there about a month, and I don't know if it was the train itself or the horn blowing or what, but it shook everything in that house and it was about to drive him crazy.

But he claimed it was that train horn. They blow every time they come to a crossing and he was right there on a corner at that crossing. it was bad. I mean, that thing would sound off.

We went fishing one time and there were these guys out working on the tracks. They were swinging sledgehammers and had shovels, and he said, "Turn around just a minute."

I said, "What?"

"Turn around. I need to talk to these people just a minute," he said.

"What are you talking about?" I asked.

We turned around and he went back up there and complained to them people working on crossties. And me having sense enough to know, and him, too, they didn't have narey thing to do with none of that, but he was just at his wit's end. But in his defense, I believe later on, I remember hearing that train whistle, and I believe the tone, or something, had changed. It didn't make the same racket that it did. So, I sometimes wonder.

Of course, he finally sold the house. He sold it to one of his relatives. He always sold stuff to his relatives and financed it for them. He was one of them kind. But I've always in the back of my mind wondered if he didn't have something to do with the change of the tone on that train. I do know he got a hold of the president of the company one time and talked to him, and I wouldn't have thought they would have even talked to him; but he was a pretty fast talker. He called them jabbed bob trains and so maybe the president of the company felt sorry for him, and he changed the tone on them.

William

He had a small business and come the first of the month every month, he'd go around and pay his bills. He had eight or ten people he'd owe a little money that he did business with. He'd tell every one of them, "That's just too jabbed-bobbed high. I ain't paying that." Every one of them would drop it down a dollar or two. So, when he got back to the house and figured it up, he'd saved himself fifteen or $20. That's just the way he operated.

Another time he went to the doctor about his ears. They charge him about 80 dollars and told him to come back in two weeks and they'd have the results of the test. He did and they told him they were sorry they could not help him. They charged him another 80 dollars. He told them to call the law and have him put in jail because he was not going to pay them to tell him they could not help. They let him go.

Spareribs

I told you he was stingy, and if you didn't watch him, he'd get you. One time we were having a party at my house and there was going to be a lot of us there. So, we went and bought a bunch of spareribs. It was nearly a hundred dollars' worth of stuff. He was with me, and another one of my associates was with us. And the reason I say associates is because when we got up there to pay—we'd already started drinking some. I looked around and they were gone, so I wound up having to pay for the spareribs.

Uncle

I had an uncle that was bad to drink. Seems like everybody I knew was bad to drink, but that's just the way it was. I know a lot of people that don't drink. In fact, most of my friends don't drink anymore. He was real bad to drink, and he was one of those kind who went plum crazy when he went to drinking. He couldn't even sit on a barstool. He'd slide off, like a snake. He'd just slither. He couldn't sit there. He had a small business, and he sold all kind of junk and stuff. Stuff like some old Japanese helmets and combat stuff. He got drunk one day and was mad with the city. He just took his machine gun and shot all the windows out of the buildings across the street. Needless to say, they put him in jail, and he had to pay a big fine, but he just enjoyed that kind of stuff. I think he enjoyed stuff like that.

They caught him over and over for DUI. One time he got drunk, and he pulled his car up there on the sidewalk. He had just even room to open the door going into the police station. "Here I am. Y'all can let somebody go now. You don't got to have nobody hired to chase me. I'm drunk so just go ahead and lock me up," he said. Well, they did.

Another time he got all drunked up and the law got to chasing him. He tried to outrun them and run a pile of stop signs. Finally, they followed him all the way out of town and he turned off on a road that had a little bridge on it. It was wintertime and cold. He run off the road and bridge into the water. He jumped out of his truck and hid in the water, or called it, self-hiding. And it was cold sure enough. There was one policeman in particular who he didn't like, and he was there after him. He knew who was chasing him, because they'd chased him so much, and he kept calling his name. He said, "Johnny. Where are you, Johnny? Come on out, Johnny?" And he'd just laugh.

He said that all he had sticking out of the water was his nose trying to hide from them. He'd call the other fellow by name, too. "So-and-so is an SOB." And then he'd put his head back under the water. Then the other guy would say, "Come on out, Johnny. Come on out."

He'd say, "So-and-so is an SOB."

Well, he stayed there a while and they finally gave up finding him and left. He come out and he naturally couldn't drive the truck because it run off the bridge. He walked to a house that was about a mile and a-half up from there and knocked on the door. He was about to freeze to death. It was two or three o'clock in the morning. Nobody answered, and he finally just kicked the door in and went inside and spent the night. He got up about the crack of day and left.

His house was about another two miles. He lived with his mama and he had a separate apartment he could sneak into. He walked the two miles to his house, and walked in the driveway to his house and they were sitting in the yard waiting on him. The fellow that he hated so bad said, "Johnny, I knew you'd come, Johnny! Let's go to jail, Johnny."

And he called it again, "So-and-so is a son of a bitch." They took him and locked him up again.

Uncle at the Bar

There was an old man that was always at standing about 10-15 feet behind where people are at the bar. I never saw him drinking, he just stood there. He wore an old felt hat and glasses wired together. I could not understand what he was doing. I knew his son so I asked him one day. He said, "You don't know what he's doing? He is standing there waiting for you drunks to lose money out of your pocket then he will pick it up."

My uncle always wadded his money up in his pockets when he started drinking, it hit me...he always stood behind my uncle. His son said that he made a lot of money standing there.

Fishing Diesel Fuel

I've just been rummaging through my head for some more stories on my buddies. I know there are some, but right this minute they escape me. So, I just decided I'd tell another little one on me. Well, not on me because I blamed my buddy for this, even though he won't admit to it. You ever seen anybody that's always, right? Him, and I've got a brother-in-law...well, you cannot get them to say the words "I was wrong."

They're right about everything. But in this instance, I'm going to let you decide what you think. We went down to the ocean fishing in my big boat and we had to gas up the boat. I pulled up to a station and the pump was out of order. So, me being as smart as I am, I looked over on the other side of the pump—the pump is on both sides—and it wasn't out of order. So, I grabbed it and handed the nozzle to my buddy. I went on in the store and started getting up my little bit of stuff. I had to pay for it, and we had to pay for the gas anyhow. So, we filled the boat up and went fishing.

The motor wouldn't crank, and then when it did it was just sputtering. And it finally dawned on me or him one, "You reckon we put diesel in that damn thing?"

"I don't know. I didn't put the—if anybody put diesel in it you did," he said.

I said, "Wait a damn minute now. You're the one that pumped the gas in there. I just handed you the nozzle. Well, let's just ride back up here and see before we do anything else if we did put diesel in it." Sure enough, on the other side there it was, diesel.

They shouldn't allow that. I guarantee you—well, since I've told this story several times, I've had several of my friends say they've done the same thing. Of course, he blamed me, and I blamed him.

We called up a boat company about 30 or 40 miles away. We were ready to go fishing. We drove a couple of hundred miles to get down there. They wanted to pump something out and said something about the injectors. Every time I'd been down there, which I've got several more rich ones, I'm going to put on here, I was thoroughly disgusted with the whole deal.

We finally got it where it would run, but it just was running. "I'll tell you what I'm going to do. I'm going to run this thing and if it blows up, then to hell with it. I'll just quit saltwater fishing down here."

So, we went back and put the boat in the water. Naturally, there was a crowd of people trying to get their boat in the water. They do a big business down there. It was plum embarrassing. We were smoking like an old freight train used to, it was a brand-new motor. We finally got out so we could fish. We'd go to move, and it would just crank and crank and crank, but it would finally catch up and go on.

To finish the story up, I kept adding gas to it every time I went, and it finally straightened itself out. But to this day he won't admit any wrongdoing. Now, I talked to a guy that's in the bulldozer business and asked, "I want to ask your opinion on something." I explained it to him.

He said, "Dumbo, a diesel nozzle,"—which I knew it already—"is shorter and fatter than a regular gasoline nozzle. Your friend is the one that took it, and he's the one that poked it in the boat, and he is just as responsible as you are." But to this day I have never gotten him to admit to being even partly wrong. What do you think?

Old Boat for Cost

I had another business deal with an associate. I had bought an old boat. I forget the amount that it was now, two or three hundred dollars or something. I really didn't need it, but it was a good price. So, I bought it. It just happened, the associate come by my house and he wanted it. I told him what I gave for it, and he really wanted it, so I sold it to him for exactly what I gave for it. I knew him pretty well and knew how he was.

I said to him, "All right. I'm going to let you have it for just what I've got in it. But now if you ever get anything I like I want you to do me the same way?"

Oh, yeah, yeah, he'd do that is what he said. It rocked on six months or so, and he picked up an item and it just happened it was about the same money as mine was on the boat. I didn't really want it all that much, but of course I would take it. But I'm kind of slow on my feet. It takes me a little while. I've seen people that you can say something to them, and they've got an answer right quick. I've never been that way. I can't come back with anything. It takes me until the next day for it to finally run through my dumb mind.

So, in a day or two later it hit me, I thought, *well, this will be a good time to test him.* So, I went to him and said, "You still got that ring?"

He said, "Yeah."

I said, "I'll tell you what I'm going to do. I'm going to take it. What do you want for it?"

He told he wanted, like five or six hundred dollars or something like that.

I said, "No, no, no. Don't you remember? I sold you that boat for cost, and our agreement was that if you had something to sell that I wanted, you'd let me have it for cost."

He claimed he couldn't do that. His was worth more than mine.

I said, "Yours is worth more?"

He said, "Yeah, mine is worth more than yours. " So much for associates.

Truck Driver Makes Coffee—MAJOR

This man I knew was a truck driver by trade. One time he was driving a truck, and he made a lot of out of town runs and was gone several days at a time. He said that after he got married, he'd call in up the road before he came home and she'd say, "Hurry on in. Come on in now, Darlin'. I'm ready."

He'd beat it to the house just as fast as he could, and they'd get in that bed. The only thing they got up for was to make coffee. He don't think they even eat nothing the whole time he was home. Well, that went on a trip or two when he came in and every time, he'd get up to make the coffee she'd say, "Hurry up and come on back to bed, Darlin'. I'm ready."

He'd make the coffee and go jump back in the bed. He said that last time he got up, she said, "Where you going, Darlin'?"

He said, "I'm going to make us some coffee."

"Well, hurry back, Darlin'. I'm ready."

"Okay." He went to making the coffee, and he was making a good bit of racket, but left there with his britches in one hand and his shoes and everything else in the other hand and he stayed gone that time three months.

And he'd tell those stories. He was a little bit different. He'd tell it and laugh and just tears would run down the side of his eyes, it would be so funny to him.

Major & Odd

They called him Major—some called him Sarge. He was a tall, slim fellow, had kind of a big belly and a little bitty head. And he had a cousin or something and his name was Odd. I think it was O-d-d, Odd, and he was Odd and lived up to his name.

This first story on him is way back yonder when they first come out with metal detectors. Oh, he loved to order stuff out of them magazines. He was a truck driver so he ordered him a metal detector. Boy, they took that thing around a time or two and he found a nickel and a dime and such as that. They went out there on this fellow's property with that thing. There used to be an old house there, and he started going all over with it, him and Odd. They hit a place, and I mean, it just went to paying off sure enough. I mean, that was just it.

So, he told Odd, "Odd, we've got to have some shovels for this job. I think we've hit the motherload."

Boys, they went and got them some shovels and went to digging. They wound up digging a hole so deep that Odd had to get down in the hole with a shovel. They had to put a ladder in there, and he would tote the dirt half-way up the ladder and hand it to Major. Major would throw it out. And he'd hand Odd that metal detector, and Odd would take that thing and put it down in the bottom of that hole and it would go to raising sand.

Major told him, "Odd, we have hit the motherload!"

They dug and dug until they were just slapped plum give out. They just finally gave up. The fellow that owned the land knew what they were doing. They went over to the service station which was the place where they gathered up and talked. He went in one day and said, "Major, did you and Odd find anything?"

Major said, "No, we didn't. We dug till we give out, but we know it's down there. We just can't get to it. Have you got a piece of equipment we could borrow to dig deeper in that hole?"

He said, "No, I don't believe I do."

So, Major said, "Well, I guess we're just going to quit."

He said, "Hell, no, you ain't going to quit."

"What do you mean?" Major asked.

"You've got to cover that damn hole up," he told him.

Major said that he and Odd hadn't even thought about that. It took them two or three months to get that hole covered back up.

Major Best Friend

Another story on Major is a good one. He got married one time. He said, "I learned something the hard way."

"What's that, Major?" I asked.

He said, "Don't ever let your best friend move in with you."

I said, "What?"

He said, "Don't ever let your best friend move in with you.

"Why?"

He told he was working at one of them plants, working the night shift and his friend had lost his job or something and didn't have anywhere to stay, so he let him move in with him. He said that his wife would always be in the bed when he got home from work.

He went home one night, but he didn't have the key to get in his house. He knocked and knocked and finally got her woke up and got her to the door. That went on two or three nights until he finally got the key from her and had him another one made. So, the next night he tried unlock the front door and there was a chiffon robe or something in front of the door.

"Well, I'll be damned. What's that doing there?"

He went around to the back door and opened it up and there was something in front of it too. It dawned on him that there must be something going on. He finally pushed his way in and they were in his bed asleep.

He said, "I run her off."

Car Man

There was a guy in my town that sold old used cars. He had them old Buicks, them old long cars, and they burned so much gas way back then with that fluid master drive, he'd sell them things on credit to people. I guess he was the first one to ever have cars he sold on credit like that.

He was a little short fellow and wore a big, ol' flat hat. If you ever notice the little men, they like to wear big hats and drive them big trucks. He sold them old used cars. He was a good salesman. He was a fast talker and shot a lot of bull. It was way back yonder when things were different than they are now.

The Internal Revenue Service came down there to check on him one time. He asked him, "Mr. Smith, I need to see your records."

He said, "Yes, sir, I've got them right here. Step out here to my office."

They walked out in front and he flipped up the trunk of one them big Buicks. They've got big ol' trunks on them. I've heard a man tell this over and over and every time he'd tell it he'd just cry! He lifted up the trunk and it was slam full of papers.

The Internal Revenuer said, "Mr. Smith, I need to see so-and-so."

He said, "Yes, sir, I'll get it right here."

He went to digging through that stuff, and on top of that the old trunk had leaked and the stuff was about half wet. It took him a while to find this paper and then he'd find that paper. All the time he was digging through them papers, he was telling about how tough it was. He was telling him that he had six or seven young'uns and just how hard it was to put food on the table and pay the light bill and all that. The Internal Revenue Service man stood around about half a day, just from one foot to the other, just about to pee in his britches. About dinner time he said, "I'll tell you what, Mr. Smith. I'm going to go on and leave you alone. You tend to your family the best way you can!"

Low Gear

I worked with a fellow in a mobile home plant. He was sort of a supervisor or something, but he really didn't do anything. I've never seen anybody as slow as he was in my life. I don't see how he held his job. He had to have been somebody's brother-in-law or uncle or something because he sure didn't earn his money. I asked him one day, when I was cutting up with him, "Have you got another gear?"

He said, "I sure do, but it's so slow I hate to mess with it."

Mex Doll Gen

I went to Dollar General the other morning, going to get a couple of things, and it was raining a little bit, drizzling rain. I wasn't in a big hurry and was sitting there gathering my thoughts. The next thing I knew I was asleep, I guess. I woke up and went on into Dollar General and came back out, and my darn battery was dead. I had left my lights on and it had killed my battery. I said, "My Lord! I thought my battery was better than that."

I looked at the time, and I must have slept for two hours in the Dollar General parking lot. Well, there wasn't anybody out but a couple of little cars. I had some jumper cables, but I knew they wouldn't try to crank me up. So, I said, "Well, I'll be damned. I'm going to have to call my wife to come up here and she's going to give me hell." I was dreading that thing.

About that time two Mexicans come pulling up in an ol' beat up pick-up truck. I hollered and told them, "I'll pay y'all to jump me off."

They said, "Okay."

They came driving up and jumped me off. I reached in my pocket for money and they said, "No money, no money." I said, "What?"

"No money."

I said, "Well, thank you very much."

While in the store, I had bought something heavy, and their help was gone on a service call. I said, "Well, I'll be dogged!"

I wanted to take it home with me right then, but I couldn't because it was too heavy for me to pick up. I was trying to decide what to do and two Mexicans come pulling up in a car. I thought, *Well, I'll ask them.*

So, I let them finish conducting their business and when they started out, I said, "Will y'all help me just a minute?" And they didn't even understand English, and I kind of pointed it to them and like pick-up, pick-up. And one of them run over there, he picked that thing up like it didn't weigh nothing, threw it on his shoulder and put it in the back of my truck. And I reached for my billfold to give them some money and they said, "No money, no money."

I said, "What?"

They said, "No money, no money."

I said, "Well, I be dog! I thank you very much."

That's the second time that I've had Mexicans help me.

MUTT & Jeff

We did some work for a man out of town on his air conditioner. And this MUTT could do most anything. Something about furnishing him some stuff and putting him in some duct work. It was a pretty good job, and it lasted two or three days. He made it through that all right, and we didn't drink a drop, we were doing real good. We went the last day and finished it, and the man paid us. He lived out in the country. We got to the first town and had to stop and buy us a case of beer. As we started home, I said, "I didn't tell you, that thing is going to blow up if he turns it on."

I said, "What?"

"I didn't tell you, but that thing will blow up."

"What are you talking about?"

"It's got the wrong orifices in it."

Orifices, I understand, is a thing that comes on if you've got to use a gas furnace. There's a different kind of orifice for natural gas or LP.

"It's got the wrong kind of orifices in it. If he turns that thing on, it'll blow up."

I said, "Well, can we get them?"

"Well, it'll be tomorrow before we can get them."

"Why didn't you just tell the man that and we'll go back tomorrow and put in the orifices?" I said.

"Dumbo, I had to have the money," he said.

"You ain't got to have the money. All you're going to do is get drunk."

"I know it! I know it, but we can't wait another day. I've got too! I'm not going to drink much. I've just got to have one beer, or two."

And he'd already drunk two or three when he told me that. So let me just say, that was our last business venture.

Let me add to the story a little bit. It was kind of cold and the man wanted to try his new unit and see if it would work. He turned it on that night and guess what? It blew up and burned every one of the wires out.

I got MUTT to go back, believe it or not, we went back over there and had to re-wire that thing inside the unit. All in the world we'd have had to do was leave that thing alone till the next day and none of that would have happened. It took us longer to re-wire it than it would have taken us to have left it alone and waited one more day, but he couldn't do that. He was just so nervous he had to have a beer.

Business Upstairs—MUTT

This one is on another one of our business ventures. His mama worked for a business uptown and they needed some work done. It was a pretty good little job that would have taken us a week or something normal like. Anybody that's normal, it would have taken about a week.

We got started and got about half-way through and got us a draw. By the way, we were working upstairs. The building had a downstairs and an upstairs. His mama and another woman worked downstairs. He knew that woman. They went to the club together a little bit. They knew he drank, but they thought he'd be all right to do the job, especially since his mama was downstairs.

It wasn't going to take but a week to finish so they gave us the job, which was a terrible mistake. We got about half through with the job. You get a draw when you get half-way through. Well, you know what that means. You're supposed to stop and get drunk and spend the money before you go back to work. Well, he didn't want to do that.

He wanted to go back to work. We went upstairs in that building. Bear in mind, his mama and the woman running the business were downstairs. He got to drinking up there and sticking his head out the windows and whooping and hollering and carrying on. They'd run up there and tell us to hush and be quiet. That went on for a while. It finally took us about three weeks to finish the job. It was just a good place for him to drink and he enjoyed it so good. His mama down in the bottom would just fuss and raise sand and carry on, but it didn't bother him narry bit. It was mainly him. He just got up there and hooped and hollered and showed out for about a week. I think that might have been our last business venture together.

MUTT & Jeff Crab Traps

MUTT and Jeff were crazy about the water. They would get an old boat or motor but never at the same time. They would have to sell one in to the other so they could get drunk. They decided they were going to start crabbing. They always wanted to get down there to the ocean, but they never could get up enough money to go. This time they decided they were going to go into the crabbing business. They got them a bunch of lumber and got in the back yard and built crab traps. They must have been ten, 15, 20-foot high. I don't know how many of them there were, but probably a hundred, or two hundred of them. They were going to get them a boat, but finally, when they sat there for about two years, they finally just burned them up.

Dumbo & MUTT Fighting

One night we went to a dance out of town. We all took our wives with us that night. And like I said, MUTT's wife was pretty rough herself. She had an old boyfriend call her and ask her to go the Bahamas. Oh, and she got to drinking and running that mouth about how she could be over there at the Bahamas drinking Crème De Menthes, and all that kind of stuff. MUTT had gotten aggravated with her and wouldn't dance with her. So, she sat there all night long and he wouldn't dance. He just got madder and madder and madder. She just rubbed it in on him sure enough.

We started home and got about half-way there. They closed the place down on a New Year's night I believe, and it was a pretty good ways to our home. And we were all drunk.

We got out in the middle of the woods and she reached over and snatched the key out of that damn car and got out and run and hid in the woods. We called and called and begged and pleaded and finally got her to get back in the car to go on home. When we got there MUTT came up in my face. After all those years and putting up with all that junk I had put up with, and the fact that he tried to fight me several times over the years, he got in my face.

That particular time, I had just had it. I beat the living hell out of him. He ran in the house and I was scared of whether he was going to get a gun or something. I was a little scared of what the other fellow standing there would do. Whenever you get people excited, you don't know what they're going to do. So, I told my wife to get in our car right quick and let's go. He didn't come out of the house for a week. He was all bruised up. But I finally got to give him what he needed.

Big Fist—Dumbo

I told you that MUTT, the little guy, thought he was tough. Well, he was kind of like a dog fight, seeking a big dog on another dog. He and Sneakie were both smaller than me, but we still like to go to a dance, and we went to lots of them.

One night, about eleven o'clock, there was this big guy who come walking over to the table and the first thing I noticed about them all was his fists. They'd have them big ol' fists because his weight was about 200 or 250 pounds. I ain't near that big. My so-called buddies happened to be gone to the bathroom He'd walk up to me and said, "I hear you want to whip my ass."

I'd have to wiggle and talk myself out of getting whipped. In fact, I did get whipped a time or two and all because of them two guys. They'd always want somebody else to fight where they wouldn't have to.

Fly Rod—MUTT

I don't know if any of ya'll are familiar with a fly rod or not. If you're a fisherman, you will be. I can't use one. It takes a hundred yards to throw that thing and you've got to throw it back and forth, back and forth. Well, MUTT had one of them. His wife loved to fish, and sometimes they'd take one of my other friends with them. He loved to throw that fly rod, and when he did it was just in everybody's way. You couldn't fish for that fly rod. He was just constantly throwing it forwards and backwards, and then drinking, if you've ever fished any, you can just realize what a mess it was. He'd hang that thing up in the trees and they'd have to go get it. He'd got it in his wife's hair once. He'd always hook them here and hook them there. It was just an aggravation. And my other friend and MUTT's wife, wanted to get rid of that fly rod so bad they couldn't hardly stand it. But they knew he just loved it so good. Oh, he just had to use that thing. Every time he did that, they'd wind up fighting before they got through fishing. I can just imagine a man trying to fish with a fly rod with two people in the boat with him. But of course, they were all drunk and they didn't really care.

    They got back this one particular time and were going to take the boat out of the water. They got all their stuff out and got ready to leave. MUTT got in the truck to do something, and he had laid that fly rod down behind the truck and he backed over it. My other buddy and MUTT's wife, boy, did that thing tickled them to death! He broke the fly rod! There ain't no way to repair one of them things, and they're right expensive. They thought they were going to get by without a fly rod for a while, but he stopped the truck and looked back there and saw his fly rod. I mean, he just jumped right straight in the air two or three-foot, and hollered, and screamed, and cussed, and carried on. I mean fire came out of his tail three feet long. He said they should have been watching him and ya-ya-ya. They said that they were glad to just stand there and take it because they knew that the next time that they went fishing, they wouldn't have to fool with that fly rod.

MUTT'S Wife DUI

My mind seems to be working pretty good this morning. Sometimes it's overactive and sometimes it's underactive, but it seems to be working pretty good this morning so I'm going to tell you another little quicky.

I had more to do with MUTT than I had to do with the others, so they'll be a few more on here about him. MUTT had a wife that was as tough as he was, and they both loved to drink. They loved the river. Oh, they loved the river, well, for two reasons. One reason was for drinking. You got drunk if you went to the river; it was just mandatory. And the fishing was second. One was just as tough as the other. They'd fuss and fight and they just loved it. One night they went out to the club and closed it down. They started home and were nearly to the house and a car got right up on them. She peeped in the mirror. She was afraid it was the law and they were going to get them for DUI. It wasn't the law.

"That's not the law," MUTT said.

"Why are they following so close? They ought not to be doing that."

"They don't need to be following that close. Well, let's just pull over and beat the hell out of them," MUTT said.

His wife said, "Let's do that! Just pull over. Pull over right here."

They pulled over side of the road and got out and guess what? It was the GBI. They took them to jail and locked them up for DUI and got her for resisting arrest or something, She showed out bad sure enough. So that cost them more money, but they dearly loved it.

MUTT & Wife Honeymoon

Come to think about it, they were married. They got married on the river. I forget the name of it. They got married on the riverbank and when they got married, they were already drinking. They didn't have a honeymoon. They just pitched a tent up there. They had their old boat and they just stayed up there and had about a three-day drunk. They said that they just had a wonderful honeymoon.

Panic Car

I bought an old car the other day. Usually after the first day when you buy an old car you have to buy another battery for it. I went up there that Monday morning and it had been real cold and I said, "Well, I better go by and check and be sure it will crank up in case somebody wants to drive it." So, I got the key and opened it up and cranked it and it run plum good. I turned it off and went to get out of the car and the door was locked. I said, "What in the world?"

So, I had to crank it back up again and it wouldn't turn back on. So, I was just stuck right there in the car and it locked. I'd never driven the car before but once, I think, when I bought it. I mashed everything I knew to mash and turned everything I knew to turn. The only good thing about it was there was a locksmith that was working right there on the same lot I was on.

I said, "Well, worst case scenario I can have that lock man to come over here and get me out of here." I didn't think. I guess I could have called the police but I panicked, and I did everything I knew to do. I mean, I thought that I was smothering to death.

I said, "Well I'll just blow this horn and that lock smith will look over here and he'll come let me out of here."

I blew and I blew, and I blew, and nobody ever came, and for some reason I just got scared to death. The only way I could figure to get out of there, was I had on my old heavy boots and I said, "Well, maybe I can kick the damn window out."

Of course, I told one of my associates about it and he said, "Well, what you done, you should have kicked the windshield out. That's cheaper."

I told him, "You don't give a damn about the cheap. All you want to do is get out of there and I'd have kicked the damn window out in just a minute."

I don't know what happened, but all of a sudden, I heard them door locks click, and I opened the door. I ain't never been so proud to get out anywhere in my life and when I did, I called over to the lock man. "When you get a chance come over here and see if you can get this car to turn on."

He said, "Sure." He come walking over there, he just turned it on and cranked it up right quick. And he turned it on two or three times and cranked it up right quick.

"How in this world did you do that?" I asked.

He said, "Well, sometimes you have to wiggle the steering wheel."

Then it hit me! I've had my car to do that once or twice, and I just wiggled the steering wheel and it would crank up. But when you're in a strange situation and you don't know nothing about the car, it's just different. And that thing scared me to death.

Red

Red was a different kind of a fellow. I really liked him. Don't know why they called him Red. I won't say he was a con man. I would just say he was fast on his feet, and he knew how to live in any type of situation. In other words, it would be hard to starve him to death. He just knew how to live.

I'm going to start off the stories the way it started. I knew him and his mama and his daddy, from years back. He went in the service. And his brother told me that Red had a high IQ. He was in the war and was wounded, and he wanted to go back, and did. His brother said that he never stayed in any one place for any length of time. He said that it was because of the service. All the things that he saw and did. Same as it did for a lot of these veterans. It kind of messed his mind up some. The way his brother explained it was that Red was running from himself. Sometimes I think I do that.

Red got out of the service and came back and started selling Singer sewing machines. Way back there when, they used them old sewing machines that you had to do the pedal. That's many years ago. Red was a top-notch salesman, and he was selling the punk out of them. The only thing was, he wasn't turning the money in. He wound up going to prison for a year or two for stealing the money.

He got out and far as I know he never worked anywhere else again. He was kind of a swapper and a trader. He was good at buying and selling. He never owned a car that didn't have "For Sale" on it, and they would always be old, selling for three, four, five hundred cars.

He always wore a cowboy hat and a vest and one of those little bolo ties, and boots. He was always decked out. I won't say he was dressed immaculate. He was everyday dressed, but he was just a sporty dresser. He always had a young, good-looking woman with him. He'd have different ones. He said that he sold a lot more stuff with a pretty girl with short shorts on with a low-neck top on.

One of his ways of making a living was with a black velvet board about eight, ten inches long and five or six or eight inches wide. However, wide as it was to hang a necklace on, he had three or four gold necklaces on it. Of course, they weren't real gold. He'd buy that stuff by the pound and it would turn your arm green in about three days. He'd buy it and the girl would put them together. She would string some through different color beads. And he'd have some that would have marijuana on them, or deer or a cross on them and this that and the other. I asked him one time what those things sold for. He said, "Dumbo, it's according to what kind of shape you're in that day. They run anywhere from five dollars to fifty dollars, according to how broke you are."

He told me once that if you ever got in a tight spot, all you had to do, was go to a church and they would give you spending money, and also gas and food. So, there wasn't no reason for nobody to starve. If you were needing something bad or had to have some money for something, there was two or three places that was real hot spots. Just go to the worse section of the town that you can find and hunt up a laundromat. You had to do it on busy days. And if you didn't have any money, just lay your clothes up, or put them in the washer. Lay that board up there, just act like you was fixing to wash. He said, "When them women saw them chains, before I leave, I have a few dollars in my pocket."

He also told me that if you could get to—I don't know what they are now, but one of these motels, like Holiday Inn, you could get back there in the back room where those women were washing those clothes. He said, "All I got to do is just go back there and just take that board out and lay it up on the washer. Just lay it up there and be friendly to one of them and start talking, preferably a stout one they are the most jovial. They'll see them chains and they'll drive them plum crazy and before you leave there, you'll have some money in your pocket." He was a very good conversationalist.

Another place he said that was a real good spot, was a restaurant, like a Huddle House or something, where they've got waitresses go in and order you a cup of coffee. If that's all you had money for, just lay that board on the table. He said that before he left there, he'd have some money in his pocket.

He just had lots of angles. And like I say, he'd buy an old car and drive it and put a "For Sale" sign on it. If somebody wanted, he would sell it on the spot, get his bags out and he and the girl would leave there walking looking at the classified ads for another one. He was just real good at what he did, and he went all over the United States doing like that. He wouldn't stay anywhere long. He had a good eye for buying and selling.

One time he came back home and opened up a junk shop. That was back before the pawn shops, and he had a lot more used item things, and he was doing what looked to me like a booming business. I went in one day and he said, "Dumbo, I'm leaving this evening."

"What?"

"I'm leaving this evening."

"What are you talking about?" I asked.

"I've got to go. I can't stay here," he said.

"What do you mean?"

"I'm closing this damn thing down."

"What in the world? You're doing good with this," I said.

He said, "Yeah, I am. I've been in one place too long. I've got to go."

Sure enough, I went by the next day and he was closed and everything in there was gone. I don't know what he did; whether he give it away or put it in one of his old cars or what, but he was gone. I didn't see him again for about six months. He went to these flea markets in these bigger towns and he'd sit there and sell stuff.

I saw him a while back. He's got to be an old man now and he's in a wheelchair, but he had a good-looking young woman with him. He was selling them kind of turquoise, Mexican belt buckles, for $60 or $70 a piece. While I was there, he sold one or two and he'd just wink at me when he sold them. I said, "Red, how much do you have in that belt buckle? Well, I know I have $5 in it." He was just good at it.

I admired him In a way. I mean anybody that can get out and make a living like that, and in the wheelchair. I don't want to do that. I couldn't do it; I'd starve to death. But anybody that can do it, and that's what he wanted to do, I admire him for it because he wasn't a bum and didn't beg nothing. I asked him one time, "Red, what are you going to do when you get old?"

He said, "What?"

I said, "What are you going to do when you get old? "You ain't paid in no Social Security, and you don't got any money. There ain't no way you can draw anything."

He said, "Dumbo, are you worried about that?"

"I would be," I said.

He said, "That's real simple."

"What do you mean?"

"All you do is sign up for them. Sign up for them food stamps and I can get some kind of." He named off some kind of checks. I reckon he'd done checked into all that.

"I'll just go to another state and sign up for everything. Then I'll just come back down here until my checks and my stamps and all come. And then I'll go to my post office box and get them. Hell, living ain't a problem. The government will take care of you."

I wished I'd have thought about it, and asked him, when I saw him in that wheelchair, if he was doing all that. It wouldn't surprise me a bit if he was. He was wounded in action and his brother told me that he could have been drawing a disability check all his life and he never would take it. That's right, he could have drawn a disability check all his life and he'd never take it. You've got to kind of admire that. He said that he didn't need to be paid for fighting for his country.

Red & Jr. South Florida

These two guys, Red and his buddy, Jr. thought they was Don Juans. And of course, to the older women, they did look good, all dolled up. They decided to go down to South Florida, that's West Palm Beach, somewhere where all them rich, old widow women are. And, boy, there was two of them old women just latched on to them. They were spending money on Red and JR. just hand over fist. I mean, they just had them a big time. Red said that they stayed down there about two weeks, and one morning the women had gone out to take a swim or walk. Jr. asked Red, he said, "Red, are you ready to go home? I'm ready to go home. I don't give a damn how much money they've got. I ain't never liked to have to ask a woman for nothing. I'm sick of having to ask them for money."

He said, "Yeah, I'm ready to go home. Let's go home." And they went home.

RED Going to California in his $400 Truck

Red's brother told me, and I don't doubt it at all, that Red was a real fast talker, but he was smart talking. His brother told me that he had a high IQ. He wasn't no dummy at all.

I ran into Red one day at the Burger King. He had his girlfriend with him. He said, "Dumbo, I need a car. I sold mine."

He had his suitcases with him.

"Where I can get a car?" I said. "I don't reckon I do."

I had an old work van and he said, "Well, you want to sell that van?"

The van was shot. I said, "Yeah, I'd sell the van."

"What do you want for it?"

I said, "I'll take $400."

He said, "I believe I'll take it. Let's drive it around the block."

We drove it around the block. The girlfriend waited at the hamburger place for us with their suitcases. When we came back, he said, "Well, I'll take it."

So, we went to my house and unloaded all my junk out of it. His girlfriend got in and started making necklaces. She had a sack full of stuff to go with it. He said, "Well, I'll see you in about six months."

I said, "Six months? Are you going in the hospital or something?"

He said, "No, I'm going to California."

And bear in mind, we live in South Georgia. "You're going where?"

He said, "I'm going to California."

"How you going? In this van. Red, you ain't going to California in that van."

"Why not?"

"Man, I'd be scared to go out of the county with that damn thing, really even the city limits. I told you it's shot."

"No, it'll be all right." He pulled out a 'for sale' sign out of his suitcase and stuck it in the window. He pulled his money out of his pocket and said, "I ain't got but $40."

"What?" I asked.

"I ain't got but $40."

I said, "You're joking me?"

He said, "No, that's all it will take."

I said, "Red, I wouldn't even go anywhere with $40."

"Naw, there ain't nothing to worry about. I'll see you in about six months." And they took off in that thing and it was smoking. About six months later, I saw an old car in the parking lot at the huddle house with a for sale sign on it. I walked in and he called me by name, "Come here a minute."

I walked over there. "Walk around here where you can see good," he said. I got on the side of them where they couldn't nobody else see in his pocket. He pulled out a wad of money big enough to choke a mule. He said, "I have been all the way to California. I've been up in Idaho."

He told me all of where he'd been, and what a big circle he made out there. "I run into the darndest thing I've ever run in in my life. We got out on the edge of Mexico somewhere, and there was an Indian reservation. There was two old women that had a trading post on the edge around the reservation. We carried them necklaces in and they just went plum crazy over them. They bought everything we had and asked us did we have anymore."

They drove a hundred miles and bought another bag of stuff and his girlfriend made necklaces all the way back. These old women gave them a place to stay and they stayed with them several days. He said, "We stayed until we got tired of making necklaces." He said that they would buy everything they made. They had enough money and they could just take it easy. He said that he done some swapping and trading, but he didn't have to push real hard because he already had a pocket full of money. There ain't much wrong with that, is there?

RED's Buddy

He had an old buddy who wanted to be like him so bad he couldn't stand it. He dressed like him, and he drove an old van like him. He had that old van full of all kind of old junk that he sold, like necklaces and watches etc. But, he just didn't have the ability Red did.

Red laughed and said that once in a while he'd want to trade items with him. "I'd always trade with him and I'd let him get the best of me because it would tickle him so good."

He couldn't do what Red did, but this same fellow we're talking about now, he was pretty slick, too. Somebody sold him a lot of land on credit in a pretty bad location. He got him a bunch of old trailer doors. We've got mobile home plants in our part of the country, and he got old used mobile home doors and built him a house out of them. It looked pretty good. He didn't have nothing in it hardly. He got the old scrap lumber and used that. Everybody liked him. After he got through with it, he went to the bank to borrow some money on it. The loan officer went out there with him and looked at it and loaned him around thirty or forty thousand dollars. That was a whole lot of money to him. When he borrowed the money from them, he said, "I knew when I borrowed the damn money, I wasn't going to pay it back."

RED's Happy Life

I wish I could think of more to tell about them, and I might later on. But it looks to me like they weren't ever under any pressure. Well, they might have been, but they sure didn't show it. They lived life the way they wanted too, and they seemed to be happy. I think that's what life is all about.

Bermuda Shorts

Well, I just thought of another little good one on me. At Belk's they had some Bermuda shorts on sale, and I needed some, so I went in and picked me out some. I went in there in the dressing room and tried them on. My wife was out there, and she was looking at them to see what she thought. So, I picked me out some and I went back in the dressing room to put my pants back on, and I opened up the dressing room and went in there. My pants were there, and I reached up there to put them on, and about that time a man was in the next stall there and he said, "Where is my britches?"

I looked and they weren't my britches. They were about the same color, but they weren't mine. I was in the wrong damn dressing room! Well, I grabbed his britches and stuck them out the door and said, "Are these yours?"

He said, "Yeah! Are these yours?"

I said, "Yeah!"

So, we swapped britches. I could tell he didn't like it much and we both was embarrassed. We got up there to the cash register to pay and somehow, he had already picked out a couple of pair of pants. I reckon they were under mine in the dressing room. So, when I got up there to the cash register to pay, I had two pairs of his shorts. Ain't that a hell of a mess?

On my behalf, I think they ought to have one "2, 3, or 4" or "A, B, C, D," one or the other, on those dressing room doors. Although, that probably wouldn't have made a bit of difference. I probably would have done the same thing anyhow.

Rope Not Tied

I went down to the river one afternoon by myself. I'm bad to do that. When you get to my age, all your partners are sick, or their wives won't let them go, or they've got to go to the doctor. I guess I'm just very, very fortunate. I reckon I'm one of the healthy ones left and I just ain't going to sit at home. I'm just hard-headed. My grandmama said that to me one time. I said to her, "You're hard-headed."

She said, "What?" She was 103 when she died and she had never been in the hospital.

"You're hard-headed," I repeated to her.

"I sure am. And you're hard-headed, too."

"Well, I guess maybe I am. I take after you," I said.

She said, "Well, I'll tell you one thing."

"What's that?"

She said, "Anybody that's not a little bit hard-headed ain't worth a damn."

That's my 103-year-old grandma.

I got to the river and had a good early start. Boy, the fish were supposed to be biting. I got everything done. It's hard to have everything if you're a fisherman. If you're going, don't leave the bait or don't leave your chewing tobacco or your life jacket etc. This particular time, and I don't why, but there is a rope that you use if you're by yourself. You tie it to your truck, and you tie it to the boat, so whenever you're backing it in the water, it won't float away from you, like I did that time up at the river.

I thought that I had everything tended to, but guess what? My rope wasn't tied to the boat, so it just floated on down the river. "Well, I'll be damned."

I nearly drowned the time before, so I was scared to go get it. I said, "Somebody will be here in a little bit, so I'll just sit here and wait." I thought that it was going to float to the ocean. I followed it down. It was on the other side of the river. I followed it down the river a long way. "Well, maybe it will float over to this side and with that running water, and I can get it."

It finally lodged up on the other side of the river. There wasn't any way to get there but swim, and I wasn't about to attempt that. So, I just went back up to the landing and sat down. Them damn skeeters was about to eat me up. Usually there's people fishing. This particular morning, I sat there for over three hours before anybody came, and when they did, of all things, I had to know them.

"What's wrong, Dumbo?"

"My damn boat has floated down the river. You mind going?" I said.

"Yeah, we'll go get it."

When I got back to the bait shop that's the first thing I heard. "Well, I heard you were at the river and lost your boat. Ha–ha–ha." T Then I went up into the café where my buddies go every morning "Well, I heard you lost your boat. You need to quit fishing. You're getting too old. You're dumb as hell. Ha–ha–ha."

It took about a month of that before they finally forgot about it. I had two other older friends that went the same day I did. The truck was pulled out of the water with both doors open and the truck was running. I guess they were in a hurry to go fishing. I turned truck off shut doors and went fishing. Senior citizens can screw up.

Dumbo Dentist

I worked down at this place at the beach one time when I was a lot younger, and we had this woman come in there, her husband was a dentist. We all tried to wait on her. We'd take turns because she always tipped real good. She wanted us to make her some extra good cuts. Also, if your teeth need cleaning, she'd get you an appointment with her husband and it would be free. My teeth looked terrible. And it finally come my time, and she made me an appointment for him to clean my teeth and x-ray them. He showed me an x-ray of my teeth, and I didn't have hardly any teeth left. It was all cavities. I had a mouth full of cavities. He wanted to set me up to come once a month. Not long after, I went to Georgia, so I didn't do it. They were yellow, and I was ashamed of them. I finally got to where I could afford it. So, I had them cleaned. I was dreading it because I just knew that dentist was just going to have to drill in every one of my teeth. I can't stand the thoughts of that drill. Back there, when I was a child, that was before they had all this modern equipment they've got now. I remember the dentist gave me seven or eight shots, and he just couldn't hardly keep me in the chair. I've always dreaded the dentist ever since.

The dentist cleaned my teeth, and said, "Well, you don't have any cavities."

I said, "What? What do you mean I don't have any cavities?"

"Well, I can't help it, you don't."

Then I told him the story about the dentist at the beach. It's sad to say, but we've got crooks in our profession just like anybody else has. I wish I'd have known that, or anybody known that, and turned him in because that's terrible.

Dog Pound—Suzzie

At the time of writing this, my dad is 92 years old and he lives by himself in a big house and he can't hear it thunder. Somebody broke in his house the other day and stole some of his stuff. I've been after him a long time to get a little watchdog. After the break in, he decided he would. So, I'm going to tell this whole story because it kind of gripes me every time I think about it.

I went to the dog pound walked in the back room and the very first dog I saw was a little chihuahua about six months old. I mean it barked at me when I went. I wanted that one. She signed me up for the little dog. You have to fill out an application, and I believe there's more to it than borrowing money. They have to know where you live, if you've got a chain length fence, if you've got this, you've got that, and I wouldn't be surprised if they wanted to know if you were married or not. I had to go through all that, but I just got excited about the little dog.

I told daddy I was going to have him a little dog coming. I noticed the people working there were real stand offish. They weren't friendly at all. They just were kind of no comment. I signed up and they said it will take a few days to go for the board to find out whether I was acceptable for this dog. I told her I live in a pretty good community, got chain length fences and all that, and I've got a couple of dogs, and I didn't figure it would be any problem.

I went back there about a week every morning to find out if they had decided anything on the dog, and every time they were the same way, just kind of acted like they didn't want to talk to you. I know why now.

About three weeks later I got a letter from them stating that I was unacceptable for the dog because three years prior to that—I want you to get this now—three years prior to that, I had a dog that didn't get a rabies shot. Big deal! You've got to decide—there's a little dog there that possibly could be put to sleep. Had you rather put him to sleep or had you rather give him a chance to live. That thing ran me hot, but there wasn't anything I could do about it. So, I got on the exchange show and I rounded up another dog and they gave it to me. It was a female and I had to take it and get it neutered. It wound up costing me $200 dollars or something like that. I don't know what the correct name for these dogs is, but I call it a Shih Tzu. I don't know what it is, but it's the ugliest thing you've ever seen. It's got black kinky hair and the only good thing about it, is I've never felt a dog with hair like this before. It's more like cotton or something. It's a soft hair and they don't shed.

I got the dog and took him to daddy. My sister was staying there with him. She's in and out, gone here and there and yonder. I left the dog around there about two weeks and it was working on daddy. He can't hardly get up and down the steps and he had to carry the dog outside, and he was messing up the floor all over the house all the time. Me and my sister don't get along very well anyhow. I went that morning and she said, "You've got to do something with this dog. We just can't handle it."

I said to myself, "Well, I can solve this."

So, she went out the door, and I just picked the dog up and left with it. I said, "He can't handle it and I sure don't need another dog. That would give me three and I ain't wanting three dogs."

But I took the little dog. As luck will have it, I went to a 7-11, and there was a woman in there, and I asked her did she know anybody that wanted a little dog. She said that she had a small child that something was wrong with her, she was sick or something, wasn't completely normal. She said that she'd love to have it. It would tickle her to death.

I said, "Well you've got you a dog."

So, I gave her the dog. I started on to the house and my sister called me in a little bit and said, "Where is that dog?"

"I gave the dog away. The dog is gone."

"You what?"

I said, "I gave the dog away."

"Go get that dog. We love that dog. We want that dog."

"Ya'll can't handle the dog. You're gone, and daddy just can't do anything with him. So, it was just causing ya'll a problem, so I just gave it away."

"Go get it."

I said, "I can't. I've already given the dog away."

"Go get the dog," she said.

"I probably couldn't get the dog if I wanted to," I said.

I could have handled her, but, I put the phone down. I know what it was, my sister called my wife and in about ten minutes—you know—how soft-hearted women are. My wife called and asked me where the dog was, and I said, "Well, I got rid of the dog. Praise the Lord, the dog is gone."

"Go get that dog. I want that dog."

"I ain't going and getting that damn dog. The dog has got a good home. We don't need the dog. Leave the dog alone."

"Well, it's just got your daddy so upset," and ya-ya-ya.

I said, "He'll get over it. He's 92, and I didn't realize it, but he's too old to tend to a dog."

So, she kept on and got to crying a little bit on the telephone…you know how that goes. So, I went to get the dog. I told the woman, "Listen, I hate to do this, but I've got to have that little dog back." I explained to her.

She said, "Well, that will be fine. I understand. But I've spent $40 on the dog."

I said, "Well, I'll just have to give you your $40 back."

So, that put me with—I ain't trying to keep up with it, but $240, $250 in a dog I didn't want. I took the dog home and my sister said that she was going to be gone, but after about a week she'd get the dog.

It rocked on about three weeks and I called her, "When are you going to come get this dog?"

"I can't tend to that dog. I'm gone all the time and daddy can't tend to it."

"Well, why in the hell did you tell me you wanted the dog?"

So, I've got three dogs now. I hated that dog, and that Friday night she got sick, naturally on a weekend. I took her to the veterinary Saturday morning, naturally they were closed. I went to the dog pound. She was dying. She could not even stand up and it was hundred degrees in back of the truck. No one was there. I kept calling the vet and kept going to the dog pound in vain.

Finally, it hit me. I went to a small car wash. I knew a man there, and he was a drunk. He just hung around. I told him I would give him $20 to knock the dog in head, because I could not kill him. I gave him the hammer and walked behind the building and came back and asked him, "did he do it?

He said, "Mr. Dumbo, I could not kill that dog."

I guess I should have given him $20, anyhow. I went back by the pound and there was a car there. I ring the bell nobody came, started to leave and a young lady came out. I asked her if she could put the dog to sleep, she said, "Yes."

I went in and filled out a paper, I believe it was three pages long. I am not too fond of the dog pound. We went back to the truck and she asked me if I had tried to feed or give the dog water? I told her that it would not eat or drink.

She said, "Lets try one more time."

She went and got a bowl of water and she would not drink it. She then, cupped her hands—I believe she had done that before. She told me to pour some water in her hands so she can put water under Suzie's mouth—she lapped it three times. That was like hello! She wanted to live. She gave me the vet emergency phone number. He answered the phone the first ring. I took her there. He said that she gotten some poison. He gave her some shots and told me she had a fifty-fifty chance.

The next morning, they called and told me to come get her. At the cost of $450 later, I still had the dog that put me over $700 in her. I hated her. I did not want another dog. I took her home and she jumped in my lap for the first time. After that, she became the sweetest dog, I ever had. She died some time back and I really miss her and pray for her every day.

Round Table Associates

Good morning. I'm up and out this morning, heading to the coffee shop. I'm in a little better mood this morning. Thank goodness, my anxiety eased off a little bit and seems to be doing fine. One thing about anxiety is I'll worry about a week or two, subconsciously, if it's coming back again. Like I said, if you ain't never had it you don't want. It's a real dread and scary thing and I do hope that it's over.

I had several friends that were sort of in the same category. We're small businessmen, up and coming and trying to get ahead, and some of us would meet up at the café every morning. One of my associates—I'm really not going to call this one a friend. I'm going to call him an associate because I feel like he didn't do me real good.

He said, "I wish that we could get us a round table." About ever so often, we could all get together and discuss issues. If one of us wanted to build a trailer park, or wanted to open a pizza place, or whatever we wanted to do, we could just tell it and say, 'what do you think.' Everybody give their input on it. It might keep us from making a mistake. He said, "But the only problem with that, before we know it one of them sitting over there across the table would be taking your idea away from you." That's what you call associates, ain't it?

This particular associate, had another friend, and they had gotten closer. I was called to do some work out at his place one day. It was out in the middle of the boondocks. It didn't look like it was all that good of a place for what they did. What I worked on was, and I don't know how to say it, but the customer that I had lost, was on his other friends property. In other words, he got my customer. And that's well and good. I DON'T BLAME the other guy. That's just business. When you're in competition close like that, really, they had rather you not get it, I think. I think your friends, associates, had rather see you go broke. I'm not that way. I'm not envious of people. I think deep down he might not even realized it. I don't think he wanted me to get that job because it was such a good job. It is terrible that I think that, and I sure hope I'm wrong. But that was my feelings. I did not think my friend would had done me like that.

And this associate was the type that if he got you something good, he wanted a binder. In other words, he wanted you to pay him some money. If he had some good news, I've always felt like he told his friend about it. Here's the clincher, the real clincher—his friend's brother had one in another town. In other words, this friend was acquainted with this type of business and he knew it was a good thing. He knew how to get in touch with the people through his brother. Maybe I'm wrong. I certainly hope I am. I just finally quit messing with that associate. He run into me somewhere later and asked me, and I finally told him. He claims that he didn't do it, but I've always wondered in the back of my mind. And this other fellow claims that he didn't do it, the friend, which I don't blame him. It was business with him. But the one I would be hard with would be the one that gave my customer to the other man.

Now then, I want y'all to be the judge and the jury. If you had a similar situation and one of your friend's friends took your customer from you, would it smell a little bit to you? Would you think it was underhanded or not?

Dumbo Cereal

Have you ever thought about how complicated it is to just sit down in your chair and relax? Used to, you just sat down in your chair, and if you liked to read, you'd get a book or the paper and that would be the end of it. But now-a-days, you have to have something to drink, and have to have the landline telephone, and now, my cell phone. And then I have the TV remote, and then I've got a remote for my heater. I have one of those electric chairs that's really convenient, and I have to have the puncher to that. Also, I have a tablet that I read now, and be sure to get your spoon. It gets to the point that there's no way in the hell for an 80 year old to get it all together at one time. When you finally sit down you will have left your spoon, your napkin, our something else and by that time your cereal is soggy and it just gives you out to finally sits down in your chair. I have changed my TV antenna. I have two punctures for that. So, that complicates even more.

Another Associate

This is another of one of my associates. I thought we was friends, but I've learned. I guess I should be ashamed of myself, but I've learned over the years you don't have friends; you have associates. And don't ever tell any of your business or your personal secrets to anybody like that because they'll wind up biting you in the tail.

But anyhow, this particular one, we were in about the same category. We talked really too much about our business and he pretty well knew mine and I pretty well knew his. We were about neck and neck. That creates a jealousy, I think.

Anyhow, I had a company come to me, and offer to lease my buildings for a very, very, very good price. We were all the way down to the short rows. So, me and my associate was riding around one day and I told him, and I saw his eyes light up. I said right then, you know, I should have kept that to myself. Well, we were down close to having the thing fixed and all of a sudden, they quit calling me.

I didn't want to call them because I didn't want to seem overanxious. I waited a week or so and didn't hear anything from them, so I called them, and they wouldn't answer the telephone, wouldn't answer the telephone, wouldn't answer. Well, finally after so many phone calls, it finally dawned on me that they didn't want to talk to me, so, I quit calling. That was a disappointment because I thought I had done it with them, and it was a real good thing for me. It costs me $240,000 for ten years.

Anyhow, this particular associate, he had another friend, and they had gotten closer. I got called to come do some work out at his place one day. It was out in the middle of the boondocks, and it didn't look to me like it was all that good of a place for what they did, but anyhow I got out there and what I worked on was. I don't know how to say it, but the customer that I had lost, well, he was on my other friend's property. In other words, he got my customer. And that's well and good. That's just business, you know. But under the circumstances, with me telling my friend, and then him and the other guy being friends and whatever.

When you're in competition close like that, really, they had rather not see you get it, I think. I think your friends, associates, had rather see you go broke. I'm not that way. I'm not envious of people. Well, I have been but I'm going to tell you about that in the next one.

But I'm not envious of people, but a lot of people are. I think down deep, and he might not even had realized it, I don't think he wanted me to get that job because it was such a good job. And that's terrible that I think that, and I sure hope I'm wrong. But anyway, that was my feelings and whenever I saw that, when I went out there and did that work at that place, it was kind of like Hello…meaning that my friend had done my other friend like that.

GPS

When you buy a new car, you need to be sure and get you one with a GPS on it. That's the handiest thing you have ever seen in your life. It'll take you anywhere in the United States, and I reckon it will work everywhere else, too. You just punch in there where you want to go, and it'll take you. And another thing, it's time consuming. While you're on your route you can play with it, and it'll take up your time and sometimes when you get there. Like the other day when I went to the Red Lobster. We played with it all the way over to the Red Lobster, and we got in the parking lot and all of a sudden it come on and said, "You have reached your destination." We started home and hit 'go home' and we played with it all the way home. When we finally got home and pulled up in our driveway it said, "You have reached your destination."

That is one handy thing! And if you don't understand that GPS, get out your owner's manual and read it a while and it's time consuming and very informative, and you'll enjoy it. But if you decide you want to go anywhere and you need to be there on time, you need to take about a ten-year-old to an 18-year-old child is what I would believe would be best, and let them run it for you 'cause if you don't, you ain't going to get there. I knew a guy that went on vacation with his wife. They were about 65 years old and they were using a GPS. He thought she would know how to work it so he took a nap. When he woke up, he was in another state.

So, they had to go back, but when they finally got there, it came on and said, "You have reached your destination."

Dumbo Cell Phone

My next one here is going to be a gripe with the cell phone companies. You can swap or change anything you want to, and the same way with the cable TV and the DISH and all that, and it winds up all being about the same difference. You try to save a dollar here, a dollar there, but I don't think there's nothing much to it. I was with a company for 20 years or longer and I had a bag phone in my truck, and it worked real good, and it was way stronger than these little small ones. I could take it down to the ocean and to the places that the other guys cell phones wouldn't work, but mine would work fine. We could call out on mine. And I liked it, but they kept threatening to cut it off.

I don't know what they called it, some kind of word for it. They was going to cut them off, going to do away with them. It got to worrying me and so I got another kind of phone and they cut that one off, I kept my bag phone, but it wasn't no good because it wasn't hooked up. I live seven or eight miles out of town and live on a small lake, and I love to fish. I had men working for me. Once in a while, I'd get off and stay gone, if we had everything going smooth, and I'd go fishing. Well, guess what? My darn cell phone wouldn't work out in the lake, and in a lot of other areas it didn't work.

The type of work I did, we did work all over the county. I kept that thing the first day, and I may have kept it the second day, but I took it back, and said, "Listen, this thing won't work. I'm working people and I've got to have contact."

It was with the same company, so I said, "Swap me back to my bag phone."

They said, "Oh, no, we can't do that. No!"

I said, "You can't?"

"No, no, no."

I said, "Well, I'll be dogged."

I said, "Man, I hate this. I can't even use my telephone."

I went right across the street to the competition and asked them, "Can y'all hook my bag phone up?"

They said, "Yes, sir."

They hooked me up to my bag phone and I kept it for a long time. I carried the little ol' cell phone back to another company. I wanted to tell them what to do with it. I told them I didn't need it and they said, "Well, sir, you're under contract."

I said, "Contract?"

They said, "Yes, sir, you're under contract and you're going to have to–"

I said, "No, I ain't doing a damn thing. The phone don't work and I'm not paying y'all nothing."

Oh, boy, that thing rocked on. it was a year longer or two, every day calling a time or two, about it. My wife kept saying, "Go ahead and pay them."

I said, "I'm not paying them. The phone didn't work. They could have hooked me back up just the same way as that one did across the street and they'd still had my business. On top of that, when you've got a customer, you've had for 20 or 25 years and they draw a draft out of their checking account, that ought to throw up a red flag."

I'm in business and I wish all my customers would have been like that. I wouldn't have lost as much money as I did. Alot of people didn't pay me. That's a win-win looks to me like and they just let me go like I was nothing,

But I kept saying, "I ain't paying them."

It rocked on and rocked on. Oh, and what they do? They said, "Well, we're going to ruin your credit—ruin your credit."

I said, "Listen lady, I don't give a damn if you ruin my credit. I've probably got more credit that you've got, and it's with Credit Line. I expect I can borrow a right smart more than you can. I don't give a damn. My credit is A-1. I don't give a damn if you do mess my credit up. And it needs messing up a little bit."

You don't ever think about these things, but my situation is different. I didn't have to have credit. Of course, one day down the line, if I have to borrow any money they might have it against me, and then all I've got to do is explain it to them, and that will wind that up. What I was trying to say is—you take young people, like maybe you that's reading this thing—people anywhere from 15 years old and up to 25, 35, 45, 50—that's got to have credit, well, they've got you by the balls, and it ain't right.

Say for instance, you were to get a phone that didn't work where you lived or circumstances, say you were losing your job or get sick or anything, and had to quit with the telephone. "Oh, three-year contract, yeah, a three-year contract and we'll ruin your credit, ruin your credit!"

Well, young people that doing anything so to have credit, they're going to pay it whether they like it or not, and that ain't right. I've been in business for 40 years and you've got to use some common sense. All situations are different, and I've said a lot of times, and people don't like to hear me say it, but rules are made to be broken.

Someone told me, to call Georgia public service commission or something similar and complain to them. I did. They answered the phone on second ring, and could understand what they were saying, and they were very cordial. She laughed when I told her my problem. She said that she had another complaint the same day. She said that I would hear from the phone company in a few days. The next day, the phone company called me and apologized and they said they didn't know why I was having a problem. But I had sent in a complaint months before. She said that I did not owe them anything. And anytime I wanted to come back to them, I was welcome. I knew I was right and I stood my ground.

Debit Card

The next gripe I've got is one with them debit cards. That's another rip-off in my opinion. Of course, I am wrong, I'm sure. Y'all are going to totally disagree with this one. But most everybody I've talked to has, and mostly businessmen, like me that have been in business and dealt with people. There's an old saying, 'A bird in the hand is better than two in the bush,' and that rings true a lot of times.

I opened up a little business and they come in there wanting me to take one. I don't even know what they call them, and the machines that takes a credit card. I don't use them—you run that card through there and they don't have to have the money. Oh, that guy told me that if you don't like it, he could take it and the next day he had somebody else that would take it, and that would relieve me of my obligation. He talked like he was with the bank. I figured it would be simple if I didn't like it. I'd call them and tell them that. "Oh, you're under a contract." About a three-year contract. I owed $1,500, $2,000 to end that contract with them.

Well, I used that thing about a month. I had three customers come in there and that darn thing had charged them twice. If you've got one of them cards or any of them cards, you better check your account because it will double dip. I know they don't do it on purpose, but it will sure screw up. I can testify to that. And it makes people mad because they thought that I was doing it, just conning them, trying to get double money, but I wasn't!

So, I started calling them and telling them to come get it, and I didn't want it, I called the bank and they said, "Well, he doesn't work here. He just stops by here once in a while."

I said, "Well, I be dogged."

And that thing rocked on. Well, I finally boxed all that equipment up and sent it back to the company and wrote in there that I had been trying to cut that damn thing off and I couldn't. So, now it's cut off because I don't got the stuff, you've got it.

Oh, boy! They started calling me. "Is this Mr. Jones?"

"Yes ma'am."

She would start screaming in the phone. "You are saying yes ma'am to me and you owe us. Three-year contract—three-year contract."

I said, "Lady, I didn't have it but a month, and I don't even have the equipment. I'm not paying you for three years and me not even got the stuff. I'm telling you, I was scared of it. It was double charging people and I couldn't afford that. I was losing my customers that way."

Oh, they kept on and on. My wife said, "Go ahead and pay them and be done with it."

" I ain't going to do it."

This particular time I offered them a settlement. I said, "Listen, I'll tell you what I'll do. I'll give you (I forget how much money $500 or something), even though I don't feel like I owe you. I'll give you $500 just to settle this damn thing."

And she said, "Oh, that will be fine."

Well, bear in mind it didn't even hit me that I was talking to one of them women in a little cubby hole probably in China or Indonesia. She couldn't speak good English. She said, "That will be fine. Yes, sir, we'll do that. We'll just do that. We'll just split it."

"That will be fine. I'll pay y'all's half of it because I did sign the lease and I feel a little bit guilty, but I don't feel a hundred-percent guilty."

And she said, "Oh, no, that will be fine, yes, sir."

So, I wrote her a check for whatever it was. Everybody now has numbers. You've got to write all them dang numbers down. I thought that she gave me the contract. No.

So, I thought that was the end of it. They kept sending me letters, and so I called them one day and said, "Listen, you need to check your files. I settled with y'all and I don't owe anything." I give them the account number and she looked at it. You couldn't hardly talk to her neither because she couldn't speak good English. She finally found it and she said, "Yes, sir, I can see where you paid us that money and you requested that you wanted to pay and just wind the bill up."

"That's right, and ya'll agreed to it. I've got the contract number here."

"Well, wait just a minute and let me read this down at the bottom."

She said, "Oh, I see what it is. Your request was denied."

I said, "What?"

She said, "Your request was denied."

In other words, they got my $500 and gave me a confirmation number. I told her I wanted to speak to the supervisor. I must have made 99 damn phone calls and explained the thing to them. They said, "Well, sir, I see where you paid the money, but you still owe us."

Come to find out, it was just what I was telling you a while ago. When you talk to anybody like that, you're talking to somebody in a cubby hole in some other country making two dollars an hour. My advice is don't ever sign a lease with anybody that you can't get out of, and state it up front. And on top of that, don't ever do no business with nobody that you feel like is sitting in a cubby hole in another country. I told them people to sue me. I wanted them to sue me. I'd have gone to Bangladesh to fight that thing. I was just that certain that I was right. What do you think?

Dumbo Check Machine 1

I've got another gripe and I know y'all ain't probably going to agree with this one either, but I imagine if it happened to be your son or your wife or, you know, it's got to affect you for you to have any more understanding. But still, you probably don't agree with me, but I don't like it anyhow.

I opened up a little restaurant and people kept coming in there wanting to use them cards, like a credit card that you swipe through that thing. I don't even know what you call them. I don't use them, and I don't like them. But they kept coming in there wanting to use them cards, so I went up there and went to the bank and signed up for one of them machines. Well, the man brought me one out there and I thought it would work with the bank, you know. I didn't know it was totally different. Oh, and he gave me that sales pitch and told me it's so many years contract, he said, "But don't worry about that. If you don't like it, I can find somebody else to take it the next day."

I said, "In other words, you won't be on to me about that three-year lease program?"

He said, "No, it will be fine."

I said, "Well, go ahead and sign me up."

So, you know it costs you to use that thing, and that's one thing on it, but the other thing is people got to coming in there complaining because that machine would charge people twice. And I advise anybody that uses those things to look at their statement real well, because it wasn't us, but it was the machine or the company or something, I don't know. And people don't like that. You can explain it to them all you want to, but they think you are stealing their money.

So, I used that thing about a month. I decided that it wasn't for me. So, I called them and told them I didn't want it, you know. Oh, a three-year contract, three-year contract, yay, yay, yay. You know how they do. I've done told you on the other one about that.

And I said, "I haven't had this thing but one month. I just be damned if I'm going to pay y'all for three years for something. I ain't used but one month.

I forget what the amount of money was now, but I said, "I'll tell you what I'll do. I'll bite the bullet and I'll split this thing in half with you, that three-year contract."

"Oh, no, they couldn't do that."

I feel like rules are made to be broken and I feel like a bird in the hand is better than two in the bush. No, they couldn't do that. And anyhow, I said, "Well, you're not going to get anything."

"Oh, your credit—credit—credit." The same thing as the other one. "We'll ruin your credit—ruin your—yay—yay—yay," you know.

I said, "Lady, you're wasting your time. Now, you better take the damn money."

So anyway, I wish that they would take me to court. I would go to Bangor, Maine to court with them people. We are being taken advantage of, and like I was telling you, it's people that don't know any different or anybody that's still working and can't afford to have a blight against their credit. They've just got to bow down and pay it. But that's not right. I believe if anybody is reading this thing, and they have similar problems, and they feel strong enough about it if they'll call.

I believe that guy told me to call the Georgia Public Service Commission or something was the name of it, and if you've got a reasonable gripe they'll listen to it, and if they think the company is wrong. I don't know how and why, but they can get them on the board. But on this one, I thought that they'd quit calling me pretty quick. So, I just let it go, let it go.

My wife was telling me, "Pay it—pay it—pay it."

Well, bless their hearts, I get to talk to them twice a day, every day. They call me twice a day.

"So-and-so's Restaurant—So-and-so's Restaurant." They call twice a day and I don't even answer it anymore. I just let it ring. I can see on there, you know. And what they do, I think what they do, they sell them accounts to different companies. In other words, you're not talking to the people that sold you the machine. You're talking to somebody in a little ol' cubbyhole over in China or Indonesia or somewhere, probably making 50-cents an hour. You can't even understand what they're saying, and they can't understand you. You sure ain't going to get to talk to no supervisor or assistant manager or none of that. This has been two or three years ago, and I believe the first of this year, if I'm not wrong, they finally gave up on me. They'd have been a lot better off to have taken the money. I don't know what it was, five, six, seven, eight hundred dollars that I offered them. But this way they didn't get anything, and I don't give a damn if it messed my credit up or not.

Dumbo Check Machine 2

Like I said, I think a bird in the hand is better than two in the bush. If I had a person come in there with the same thing to me, and he was doing business with me, and had the same deal, maybe he got sick or whatever or couldn't pay, I would give him the same courtesy because you're one out of a million customers. They're not going to miss your little bit of money. I just think that in business you are supposed to have a little bit of common sense. But I'm going to give you the chance to see what you think. Would you be on my side or would you be on their side?

Denture Paste

I went to Florida fishing with three of my associates. We had two rooms, with two sleeping in each room. I got up the next morning and I'd forgotten my toothpaste. So, I went over next door and everybody was getting ready. I walked in the bathroom and had my toothbrush with me, I got me some toothpaste and put it on my teeth, and I'll be dogged. I can't think of the name of that stuff, but if you've got false teeth you use it to hold your teeth in. The name escapes me. But I can tell you what, it'll damn sure work because I brushed my teeth with that stuff, and just the time I got them brushed, it locked my damn teeth together. Boy, they liked that because, I mean, they laughed. Denture-something-or-another or something. I can't remember. But I mean, that thing tickled them. They laughed and laughed and still once in a while they ask me if I've brushed my teeth with that anymore.

State Patrol

Me and my buddies went down to the coast fishing in my truck, back when we were younger and having good times. We'd snuck off from our wives. We wound up at one of these dance clubs that night and got drunk. One of these guys, he was crazy. He'd get out there and if nobody would dance with him; he'd just dance by himself. He was hilarious. Everybody liked to see him. He was long and tall, and he'd get down on all-fours and dance around right by himself, and just laugh and carry on.

He got to dancing with a woman across the way and she asked him to buy her a drink. He took her drinks stolen off of someone else's table. Now, you talk about stingy, he was stingy. It's a wonder somebody didn't kill him.

One time, he and I were out there dancing pretty close together, and this woman said to me, "I ought to slap the mess out of you."

I said, "What?"

"I want you to quit playing with my butt or my boyfriend is going to beat the hell out of you."

"What?"

I looked around at him and this crazy guy was laughing because it was him that was doing it. He could just think up the most damn stuff you've ever seen in your life.

We had another one and I called him brain dead. He's just a big mouth, a big ol' blow. He was a painter and he was doing pretty good.

He just kind of felt himself. We stopped at the Huddle House to get us something to eat. It was about twelve or one o'clock in the morning, and everything had quietened down. There wasn't anybody at the Huddle House that night much.

There was a state patrol car parked out front, and he was parked close to the line of the parking space. I said, "Holy moly! That's a state patrol." We were all intoxicated.

So, I backed up and tried to get a little straighter in the parking place. About that time the state patrol came out the front door. He was black, which that didn't have anything to do with it, I don't reckon. He came out the front door, and about that time that fat one that felt himself. I said to them, "Don't ya'll get out of this car!"

Well, 'feel good' thought he was just bad sure enough, but he was really a big ol' baby. He said, "I ain't worried about that SOB." He opened the door. And a damn beer can fell out and rolled up under the state patrol car. The state patrolman was right there watching it.

I said, "Good God almighty, we're all going to jail."

He jumped back in the truck right quick then. The state patrol walked around to my side and said, "Tell the driver to step out."

So, I stepped out.

"I see what ya'll are doing. Have ya'll got somebody to come get you?"

I said, "Oh, yes, sir. Oh, yeah, we've got somebody." You know how it is when you're drunk, and you're thinking way out.

He said, "Well, you better not leave this parking lot. You better have somebody to come get you."

I noticed he walked around and looked at our tag and he saw we had an out of town tag, I imagine he knew where we were from. I had a place, probably four or five miles away, but there was an overpass that was right there close to the Huddle House. They get close to the overpasses with them kind of places. We sat there a few minutes.

I said, "What are we going to do?"

My buddy said, "Aw, he ain't going to bother you. You just go on."

I said, "Well, you want to drive?"

"No, no, no." I said.

"Well, I don't really want to drive either."

So, we sat there a little bit, and we decided to go on in the Huddle House. We got in the Huddle House and that fool, the one that was dancing around on his all fours, and the one that felt so good, the flat-nosed, big-mouthed one, they was the two worse ones, they got to showing out so bad, they run us out of there, and said that they was going to call the law.

We got back in the truck. I said, "What are we going to do? Man, I'll bet you a hundred dollars he's sitting up on that overpass watching us, and if we leave here, he's going to get us for DUI and public drunk or whatever."

We didn't know what to do. We sat there about 15 or 20 more minutes. Our liquor was beginning to wear off and we were ready to go home. I finally cranked up and left. The only thing I can think of, is that state patrol thought that we were heading home, which was up a major highway. If we'd have been going south, he would have gotten us. He was mad. I mean, he was mad. I don't know whether the black white issue had anything to do with it or not, but he was really mad with us.

I never have understood why he didn't lock us up to start with unless he's not allowed to do that on private property. I just don't think he was wanting to let us off scott-free because we were intoxicated. We sat there fifteen, twenty, thirty minutes and I finally cranked up. "Well, I'm sober now." We took off. I had a place about five miles away, but like I said, the overpass was right there, and he could see us. I came out and went up on that overpass and made it all the way to my place without getting caught. That's just another one of my war stories.

Low-End Help

Another story. This thing kind of ties in to that other one and is about the anxiety.

I was in a small business one time where I worked a lot of low-end help. I had this one in particular, that I didn't know that he did drugs, but he was bad to drink. He went with all the women and he was kind of a ladies' man. He was a tall, handsome-type fellow, about 6'2," weighed about 185 pounds. He was going to these stores and he didn't dread it. I mean, he'd flirt with them from the time he got in there. But whenever we'd knock off in the afternoon, if he was riding with me, we'd go by one 7-11 and if he needed beer, he'd call the cashier some sweet names, and he'd just grab a 12-pack of beer, and he'd go out the door with it. And if he needed cigarettes, it would be the same thing. Just whatever he needed. And there's a certain class woman that just really liked him.

So anyway, he worked for me and he was kind of rough and all, but he did a good job with his work. I didn't know he was doing some of the things he was doing. The first instance I had with him is we went over there to work one morning, and there was a man and his wife over there. We got out of the truck and he was madder than fire. He said that somebody had tried to run his wife off the road with an ol' truck for putting septic tanks in. They called it a rail truck. He said that somebody had tried to run his wife off the road with that rail truck that night or sometime, I don't know, and I mean he was mad. I said to him, "Well, it couldn't have been us. Mine is locked up in that gate. Ain't nobody been in it."

Oh, he carried on and carried on, and finally kept on until I convinced him it wasn't us. Why in the world it didn't dawn on me to go out there and feel that motor, I don't know. At that time, I just didn't realize he was doing all that kind of stuff. Come to find out, he was sneaking my equipment off of there if I ever wasn't around. I'd take off and go fishing once in a while. He'd take my equipment off and was doing jobs. He was just doing a lot of things I didn't know about.

But anyway, me and this fellow had been up to the river one day fishing. We'd been fishing and drinking, and we come home, and I wasn't drunk. We came home and I passed him, and he had my equipment somewhere. I went to him and said, "Take my equipment back to the shop right now." So, he did.

I'm still up there at the friend's house, me and the one that went fishing, and he come up with the other fellow's son, and he bowed up at me. I was an older man then, but he bowed up at me wanting to fight. My buddy there, he'd already had a lot of trouble with his son. They were smoking pot and all that stuff, you know, and he'd had a lot of trouble with his son. So, I looked around there, and he had him a baseball bat. His son was going to jump on him. He was a young, strong thing, too, you know, and he had him a baseball bat.

Well, his son didn't mess with him, but the other one jumped on me and I was just lucky that he wasn't a fighter. He was drunk or doped up is what he was, but he done them roundhouse swings, and he just kindly hit me side of the head. He did knock my glasses off, and I believe he did hit me one time. They pulled us apart and I went home, and I was in a hell of a mess. My wife and I was getting a divorce and I had—everybody though I had tried to burn my house, but I didn't. I didn't have a whole lot of insurance on it and it was paid for.

Anyway, my neighbor called me. I had just turned the stove on and put some grease in my pan. I was going to cook me a steak and I had just turned the grease on the pan. My neighbor called me and invited me to go eat fish with them and they had it ready right then. They lived right up the road from me, so I said, "Yeah, I'll be up there in just a minute." I went off and left the grease on.

Another friend come by there, we were all friends back in that time, and he knew we were all partying together in that neighborhood or something, you know. I was up there at the other guy's house fixing to eat fish and he come up there and he said, "I went by your house and I didn't see you there. But I saw smoke. I thought you might be cooking."

When he said smoke, it hit me that I had left that darn grease on. I went up there and my kitchen was on fire and I had to put it out. Anyway, I didn't realize that the insurance company would furnish me a place to stay and all of that, you know. I was staying in my house and the darn ceiling in the kitchen was burnt out. The kitchen was burnt out. Just lucky it was cold wintertime and didn't have to worry about skeeters and all of that.

Anyway, that's enough tragedy right there; divorce and your damn house liked to burned down. I was having trouble sleeping and all of that. I had some dogs and I lived right by myself down about a thousand foot lane or something back up in there in trees. And here that guy come that jumped on me walking down the road. I said, "Oh, hell. Here comes trouble."

So, he come a walking on down there. I had a shotgun that was loaded with 00-buckshot and I stood it up right by the door. There outside the door I had a screened-in porch, and then outside the screened in porch I had a small chain link fence. Well, he come walking up there, and the shotgun is laying there by the door and he couldn't see it.

He said, "Boss man, I want to talk to you."

I said, "We don't have anything to talk about. You're fired."

He said, "Well, in that case, I'm going to come in there and whip your butt."

I said, "No, you ain't going to whip my butt. You better not come inside that fence."

He opened the fence and took two or three steps. I was scared of him. I couldn't fight him. And he could have killed me right there. He took two or three steps and I said, "You better not come no further now." He took another one or two. When he did, I pulled that shotgun out. I was so scared I didn't know what to do. I didn't want to kill him. I said, "Don't you take another step now."

He come on again. And the third time he did it, I clicked that thing off of safety. Anybody can tell you anything they want to, I'd do this, I'd do that, they don't know what they would do. It was just instinct with me. I was shaking all over. I couldn't hardly hold a gun on him, but I had that thing pointed right on his heart, and I didn't point it there on purpose. You've heard, shoot them in the leg or this or that or the other. It didn't cross my mind. It was just instinct. I put that thing straight on him. I would have blown a hole through him big as a dinner plate.

But anyway, I said, "Now, I told you, you ain't going to come here and jump on me. You move one more time…"

I intended to do just what I told him. Well, during all this time my mind was turning over like television sets used to do, flipping over and over and over. He had a wife and two or three young'uns. I said to myself, "I'm going to kill him and I'm going to wind up in jail and they're going to take everything I've got." And besides that, a man told me, one time he killed another man. I heard him tell several people, that If there's any way in this world, you run or do something. He said he never, never overed it.

I'm a tender-hearted person and I wouldn't have neither. It would have probably drove me crazy. But anyway, all that was running through my mind while I was just waiting for him to take another step and I was fixing to kill him. I come within an eighth of a gnat's butt of killing him. And he finally said, "Well, give me a beer and I'll go on."

I said, "No, I ain't giving you a beer. You get out of here and go on."

I saw that was the only way that I could even stand a chance of reasoning with him. Come to find out, he was on dope, this crack cocaine and all of that, and he was plum crazy. I didn't know that it would work, but if that beer would get him away from there, I was willing to get him one. Where the refrigerator was, was about four, five, six steps back in the house. I run over there to the refrigerator and got him a beer. I walked out there and opened that screen door and tossed it to him out there in the yard. He stood right there in that one spot. He took the beer, and after he took the beer, he turned around and left.

I've talked to the doctor on this anxiety stuff, and I've read up on it some, and according to what they say, they think that it might be linked to a traumatic experience, and maybe that's what it was. Of course, I've had some more traumatic experiences, so it could have been one of them, too. But anyway, he left and thank goodness. He wasn't worth killing. Thank goodness, it wasn't long after that he got in trouble and he left. He was from New York, and he went back to New York, and I've never heard from him since.

I have always thought that this plus losing my family caused my anxiety. The doctors think that traumatic experience can bring this on.

John Spivey Grocery Store

There was this guy in my hometown and his son, you couldn't have got them certified because they were too crazy. Several of these people I'm talking about on these things is like that. They just ain't got enough sense to get certified as being crazy. But this one in particular, he had a son and he was always spoiled. His daddy had a store and he was the only child. He gave him pretty well whatever he wanted. He was pretty smart. His mama and daddy had a grocery store, and why they did it, I've never understood, but they opened him a little grocery store right nearly about beside them.

You'd go in there, he had a recliner in there, and he'd have some ol' potatoes in there that would be about rotten and ol' oranges and this and that, but everything would be about rotten. He'd be laid back in that chair in there. When you go in there he'd say, "Come in! Come in, Brother! Come in!"

You'd get what you wanted, and he'd finally drag up out of that chair and go up there and wait on you. Everybody went down there because it was just comical, and he was always wise cracking. He had all kind of jokes always. You say anybody that just was comical, he was. Well, anyway, they made up a trick on him one day. He wasn't married at the time and they made up a trick on him one day. They set him up! He was laid back in that chair and this big guy comes in there and said, "Are you John Spivey?"

He said, "You damn right! Who are you?"

The big guy said, "I'm the man that you've been going with his wife and I'm here to whip your ass."

They said that Orville jumped up and run out that door, just left the store, and run down the middle of the road. He left the store unlocked all day that day. He didn't even go back to work.

John Spivey #1

John Spivey was babied all his life. His mama and daddy babied him just like he babied the baby. You could ask him, "How's the baby doing?"

And he'd say, "Well, the baby is doing fine. I have got him in college. He's going be a rocket scientist."

I never knew the baby to work. One time # 1 opened up the baby #2 a liquor store right beside his mama and daddy's old grocery store. Boy, I mean the baby had a good time over there. #2 was a big, fat guy and he was just about as crazy as his daddy was. He kept a crowd of men over there all the time. Young men his age would stand around that liquor store. I went in there one day and every one of them was single and about the 25-age bracket and I said, "Boys, when y'all going to get married?"

"Married?"

"Yeah, when y'all going to get married?"

They said, "What in the world do we want to get married for? We can stand right here in this store and in a little bit some girls will come by wanting a six-pack of beer and want to know if we want to go smoke a joint. Why do we want to get married when we can stand right here in this liquor store and get all the women we want?"

His daddy opened, JOHN # 1, a grocery store when he was young. I never understood why? They were in competition with each other. They were almost side by side. Everybody liked him, and he was so comical, people would go over there and stand around and laugh and talk and cut-up. He'd be laid back in that chair. If you went in there to buy something, he'd have everything over there was out dated and he just didn't give a flip for nothing.

One day we got up a little joke on him. He's a little short fellow, and just liked to run his mouth. This fellow came in and said, "Are you so-and-so?"

He said, "You G-D right! Who are you?"

The man said, "I'm the man that you have been going with his wife and I have come here to whip your ass!" Boys, when he did, # 1 jumped up out of that recliner and ran. He left the store and ran down the road. His mama and daddy had to lock up for him. He never did come back that day. It liked to have scared him to death.

After that he got married, he had two boys. He wound-up divorcing and they had to go to court. It was hilarious. Everybody that he knew was there because they knew it was going to be a big joke because he was crazy. He told the judge, "Your Honor, how would you like it if you come home tired and give out every day and start in the house and have to pull off your shoes and go in and tippy toe around dog shit?

The judge just turned around in his chair laughing. They argued the case back and forth and the judge finally came a decision and he said to him, "I'm going to award your wife so many dollars."

He said, "Well, Judge, I'm sure glad. I'll try to give her a little bit, too."

Temple Love John Spivey #1

The old judges face turned red as a beet and he sat there just a minute and he lowered the boom on him. I forget how much money it was, but I mean he popped it to him. I always like to call his house on Christmas Eve. He had a recording come on. I can remember a little bit of it.

"This is a temple of love and happiness. Brother so-and-so and the baby lives here. If you don't have anything to do, or anything to eat, just come on over here and we'll feed you. I prefer that you be a young good-looking woman."

The rest of the time, you'd call over there and the answering machine would say, "Hello! I'm either not home or I'm on the throne. The King is on the throne. Just leave your message and I'll try to call you back later."

John Spivey #2

He got his son #2 and her son in the divorce. They had a lot of trouble with them over the years. Once in a while his ex-wife would call to get on to him. She lived about 50 or 60 miles away. This particular time, the boy's grades weren't good and the school contacted her. She called him raising hell about the boy's grades. She said that he needed to do this and that.

#1 asked, "Well, where are you right now?"

She said, "Well, I'm at the house right now."

He said, "Well, if you can just stay there about an hour. I'll send them over there and let you try."

She said, "No...no...no...no. Just do the best you can."

John Spivey #1 Preacher

This same guy I told you he was a nut. We had a restaurant we went to every morning and it had a big long table. A lot of people went in there, and we cut up and had a good time. Everybody loved to see him coming because he was always going to have some bull. If anybody new comes in, say your brother-in-law was with you or somebody new from out of town, if he spotted them, he'd sit just as close to them as possible. He would talk to them a few minutes and tell them what his name was and tell them he was an ordained minister. Then he'd flip his billfold open and show his card verifying he was an ordained minister. Then he'd talk a little further and he'd say, "Oh, by the way, I just got married. I ain't shown you my wife's picture."

Of course, we all knew what he was going to do. Everybody would be real quiet and act like there wasn't anything going on. He's tell them, "I just got married last week. Let me show you a picture of my lovely bride." He'd flip his billfold open and come out with the ugliest woman you have ever seen. She'd be missing a couple of teeth and have a wart or two stuck up on her head. Everybody would just watch the man when he was doing that, and nearly every time their face would turn just as red as a beet. We'd just laugh and had the biggest kick of that.

Reverend John Spivey #1 Goes to the Doctor

The Reverend John is the one that everybody liked so good, and he'd that cut up all the time and always had something quick to say. He called on doctors' offices. He went in this doctor's office one day and he went back to see the doctor and the doctor said, " John, I just got married."

The reverend said, "Is that right? Well, good, Doctor."

The doctor said, "Yeah, I married me a young woman this time."

#1 said, "Well, that's good, Doc."

The doctor said, "Yes, sir, every evening when I go home, she'll meet me at the mailbox. I always stop and get the mail. I like to get the mail. She'll see me out there, and she'll run out there and start kissing me and trying to hug me through the window. She'll do that all the way to the carport and then when I go inside and sit in my chair she'll just jump up in my lap and just kiss me and hug me. Of course, I'm pretty good to her. I bought her a ring, and I bought her a fur coat, and I bought her a car, and some things like, but it was all worth it if she'll just keep a-doing that."

#1 said "Yeah, Doc. That all sounds real good. Come to think of it, I've got an ol' dog named Spot that will do all of them same things for $5 a week!"

Kill the Cow

I've got one or two short ones on this guy. He had a wife that was crazy about him, but they fought and raised sand. He drank, but he was good to her, but when he'd get to drinking, he was just crazy. One time they got into it, and he got the gun out. She run across the yard trying to get away, and he killed the cow. Oh, she loved him and he loved her.

I was over there one day and she had a shovel and had boots on. I told him that I believed if he told her to dig to China, she'd get her a shovel and start digging. That's how good she loved him. And I liked him. He was a good fellow, a comical fellow.

They were having trouble with the septic tank. He had gotten sick at that time. His nerves were bothering him bad, I think. They had the septic tank opened. She had a bucket and she had dipped about half out of it. She'd hand him the bucket and he'd take the bucket and go pour it out. I said, "What are you going to do? She's not going to be able to dip all the way."

He said, "Oh, when she gets down a little bit lower, I'll just get her a ladder." He just laughed.

She said, "You ought not to make me work like this." She was just tickled to death to be there doing it!

Picking up Rocks

The same guy, W.L., that got on the dance floor and danced by himself, was hyperactive. He just couldn't be still. He used to sell insurance. We'd be at Hardee's drinking coffee sometimes in the afternoons and you'd see him pull up. He'd run in Hardee's and run to the bathroom right quick, then run up and get him a glass of water. He was bad stingy sure enough, and water was free. He run get in his truck and take off to sell insurance, then he'd run back to his house. He started him a mobile home park, and I finally told him he was creating himself a monster. He got a lot of them and he just kept adding, kept adding, kept adding. I've always thought that's what killed him. He just couldn't slow down. Here's a good for instance.

I did some work for him one day and they were digging a hole with a backhoe. I believe he was putting in a septic tank. It was real rocky dirt and he had a bucket and was going to pick up rocks, because they were all over the top of the ground. "Show me how you pick up rocks."

"What?"

He said, "Show me how you pick up them rocks."

I couldn't understand what he was talking about. "I want to see how you pick them up and then I want to show you how I pick them up."

"Well, okay." So, I bent over and started throwing some rocks in the bucket, kind of normally.

"Okay. Now let me show you how I pick them up." He took the bucket and started picking them up and it was like he was fighting fire.

He was just, throwing them in the bucket four or five times faster than I did. He said, "I just can't slow down. This is the way I pick them up."

I said, "Man, no wonder you…" That's just the way he was, and I believe that's what put him to an early grave. He died young. I miss him.

Dumbo 2

I just came back from the river. The fish bait man sold me some crickets. He said that he wanted me to promise to be careful. I told you that he calls me Dumbo. I'm so good at screwing up that's a nickname that he gave me. I went fishing and didn't do all that good, which I'm getting worse instead of better. I'm fishing more and catching less. I need to get me another hobby. I went fishing this morning and it was foggy, so I had turned my lights on. I got back to the truck and my dang battery was dead as a hammer. It's a ghost town up there where I was fishing. I got lucky. I didn't know what I was going to do. There were some people came to work on an old tractor down the road. I waved them down and they cranked me up, cost me twenty bucks. Well, it didn't cost me. I just gave him twenty bucks. It was well worth more than that. I don't know what I've have done if they hadn't come. Just another one on me!

Boat Trailer

I loaded up my boat and had everything ready and took off fishing. Everything was going real good when I left my house, thank goodness. Before I got to the main highway, it's just a paved road with a lot of traffic before eight o'clock in the morning with people going to work and school. I nearly got up to the state roads and looked back and my damn boat, was falling off the trailer. I was lucky. I have some good luck along with my bad luck. I was lucky that it came off when it did because it could have come off anywhere down the road, and it would have torn all to pieces in the middle of the road. But for some reason, it waited till I got nearly to the stop sign and it slipped off.

Well, naturally, it wasn't but just a few minutes, there was 15 or 20 cars coming behind me, and they were all peeing in their britches. It just so happened a friend of mine was back there. I knew what to do. I just forgot to hook it up to the wench, I'm good at that. I just pulled the rope out and put it to the wench, winched it up, and went fishing. It didn't even mess up the boat but a little on the back, but not enough to worry about it. It was an old raggedy boat anyhow. But naturally, some of my cohorts happened to be back there, and naturally they had to go to the bait man up and tell him, so all the fishermen heard it. The bait man said, "I'll say it again. That's why I call you Dumbo!"

Dumb Booze

I had a friend when we were about 12 or 13 years old. I don't know If you've ever heard of them, but I think they might have called them dumb buoy or something or another. They made the real ones, out of a cypress knee. They'd drill a hole in it, and put a string through it and put rosin on it, and then you'd pull it and it would make a terrible racket. They say that they used them, back in the old day, when criminals got loose and got in the swamp, they'd pull them dumb buoys. That thing makes a terrible racket. It will make the hair stand up on your head and your arms. I mean, it's just a terrible noise it makes. The real one does, I'm sure. The ones out of that ol' hollow log. They say the prisoners will come out on there on in the middle of the night.

We made us two out of some lard cans, put a string through them and put some rosin on them. You could pull them, and I mean they made a racket. Not very far from his house there was a lover's lane, and always on the weekend, there'd be one or two in there, on a Friday and Saturday night.

I was spending the night with him, so we sneaked up before dark and got on both sides of the place there where they had to park. In a little bit, here comes one cutting it through there. They turned around right quick and turned that radio on good and loud. We give them about five minutes to get started good, we pulled them oink-oink. That radio switched off and they sat there a few minutes, then we pulled it again.

You talk about cranking it up and putting it in gear and getting out of there. I think that might have been back before they had air conditioners. I mean they busted loose, just ran over them damn bushes and trees, getting out of there. We did that several times and we'd just giggle. It was funny.

The last one pulled in and we did the same thing. They backed up and turned off, but they didn't have a radio that time. We give them a few minutes and all of a sudden, he pulled his, "ohhhh," and I pulled mine, "ohhhh." About that time, the car cranked up and backed up about another ten-foot. It was woody up in there. That's back when they had antennas on cars. I heard that damn antenna whipping in the trees, and it hit me. I got to where I could see. It was the state patrol. I hollered over there to my buddy and said, "Hey, State Patrol."

About that time he pulled his, it said "ohhhh," and then he pulled it about three times there right close together. The man stepped out of the car and said, "All right, boys, come out of there. State Patrol."

Bear in mind we were about 12 or 13, and when he busted out one direction, I busted out in the other one. We were out in the country. I jumped two or three barbed-wire fences and run through pastures. He went the other way. I finally wound up way back over there in a field. I heard him calling me a way off. So I started going to him. There had been a bunch of cars come out there, I reckon State Patrol. How they do things like that?

Whenever they finally left, I went to him, and he was up a big oak tree. We got together and went back to the house. We were skint up and scratched up. That's the last time we did that. Since then, I have learned there is a federal law against using dumb buoys. The real ones must make a terrible racket. I would like to hear one.

Well Done MUTT & Jeff

Now, they were a doozies. They were a card. They were different, and they both loved to drink. And if they got an automobile, the first thing you do is, you're supposed to wreck it. You're supposed to bend it up, The guy was a pretty good handyman, and he did a little contracting, and his brother was more of a salesman than he was. MUTT was actually the one to do the work. They heard about a pretty good-sized job that was going to be done out at a plant. The oldest brother went out and sold the job. He said, "Dumbo, it was a one-way road going in there, and I had to go in the wrong way because the car was bent up all the way down one side. I had to go in there wrong where they couldn't see the side that was bent so bad."

That thing rocked on, and he finally sold those people the job. He went out the day and got the contractor on the job.

"Since I've given you this job, you ought to take me out to dinner."

"Dumbo, I had to think fast, so I told him my brother never would give me but a quarter at the time, and all I had in my pocket was a quarter."

Of course, the reason that his brother wouldn't give him more than a quarter, if he gives him a dollar, he'd figure a way to take it and go get drunk. So, I guess he was doing the right thing. I don't know what he told him, but he somehow wiggled out if it. I would have bet my pick up truck they would not have made it after the first draw. I figured they would get drunk and screw it up somehow.

MUTT & Jeff—Fish Market

The next one I'm going to tell is on two of my associates. I won't say they were drunks. I'm just going to say they really loved to drink, more than the average. And they overdid it lots of times. They went on lots of ventures and did lots of things. This is the first of several of their screw-ups. I believe one of them was worse to drink than the other. He couldn't stay anywhere long. He's from here to there and everywhere. Neither of them was married. They went over to another town close by and opened up a fish market. They were doing real good business. They were just exceeding their expectations. It went on about a month and everything was working real well.

The barber shop was right next door to the fish market. Jeff had the money in his pocket for the week. It was just before closing time. He said, "I'm going to step over next door and get a haircut."

MUTT said, "All right, go ahead. I'll go ahead and finish cleaning up, and then I'll come pick you up."

He said, "Okay."

In a few minutes, he got through cleaning and Jeff hadn't come back. He said, "Well, it must still be busy over there." He stepped over to the barber shop and the barber shop was closed. MUTT said, "Oh, hell, he's down there at that bar drinking right now. I better go get him before he gets too far along." He took off down to the bar and he wasn't there. He went by the liquor store, and they said, "Well, yeah, he had been there."

"Well, was he walking?"

They said, "No, he was in a taxi."

"A taxi?"

"Yeah, he was in a taxi when he left here."

"Well, I guess he must have gone on home. I better go on home and catch him. He'll be spent every bit of the money." He went home, and he wasn't there. He looked and he waited, but he never did show up.

About six months later, Jeff called him and he was in Miami, Florida. That's the kind of brother everybody needs, ain't it?

PT Boat

My intention when I started these stories, it was to diversify. I was going to try to mix these things up a little bit to maybe make it more interesting, so I'm just going to have to just go ahead and tell them all.

There was three of those brothers and they all loved to drink. I mean, drink. Anyway, they could screw up the worst you have ever seen in your life. They had a dream of being on the water, but they never could get a boat and a motor at the same time. It would either be an old raggedy boat or a motor. I know one time they got drunk and went down to somewhere and they bought an old PT boat, a big old boat that the back had been knocked out of it. They brought that thing home and they worked on it two or three months, trying to get the back in it.

Well, they got drunk and got in a fight. They loved to fight. And they wound up selling it for scrap. That's just the way they operated. They just couldn't seem to get them a boat and a motor at the same time. You'd go over there and they'd have an old motor in a barrel. One of them was a big tall fellow with long, big arms, husky arms, man arms. He was a big guy. You'd go over there and he'd be over there, and you could done tell he was drinking. When he was drinking, when he smiled at you his lips touched his ears. Well, I went over there that morning and he said, "Sammie, let me show you something."

I said, "All right."

I walked out there in the yard and he had that old motor there. He reached down and snatched that thing one time, and with that ol' long arm he must have pulled that thing four-foot. It hit the first leg, and I mean it was running good. He looked around at me and grinned, you know, with that ol' grin he had. He laid his head on the motor and turned around and looked at me and just grinned. It just tickled him to death.

A man and his wife worked at the river fishing in a slough and they kept hearing noise coming out of the river, cursing and really showing out. They passed by a man and a woman and he recognized them. MUTT was in the boat and Jeff was in the water trying to steer an old big boat, evidently the motor will not crank. His wife said, "Honey, do you think we try to help them?"

He said, "Hell no, and be really quiet and maybe they will float on by."

Boxing Match—MUTT

Going to the coffee shop is the high point of my day, and the other people tot. We're all retired, old, and we sit up there, gripe and groan, talk politics and jab at each other. It never gets serious and we just have a good time. I think we all thoroughly enjoy it. I'd sure hate for them to close down in the morning. I've left the coffee shop and I'm going to tell another one about those same guys, but this story is about one in particular.

MUTT was married. He was a little short fellow. Lot of times, they think they're the toughest, and he did. One night, they had a boxing match in a town close to us, and they gave prize money if anybody could stay in the ring with the guy for so long. We got to drinking that night and, oh, he said that he could whip him. He could whip him? Yeah. He was a little short fellow and he had big ol' ears. We were always aggravating him about his ears and his teeth. He had some bad teeth, so we'd give him a fit and he couldn't hardly stand it.

We went over there that afternoon, and he signed up. It cost him ten dollars or twenty dollars to fight him. It finally came his time to fight, and they put the boxing shorts on him. I swear to goodness they hung down around his ankles. He got in the ring with that guy and that guy was a pretty big guy and was all muscled up. They rung that bell and MUTT walked to the middle of that ring, and stomped his foot one time, with them ol' big gloves on. He motioned for that guy to come on.

He walked out there, hit MUTT on the nose the first time and knocked him through the ropes. You talk about getting up and gnawing those gloves off his hands! I mean, he was gnawing those strings to get them off. He got back up and we asked him did he want to get back in the ring. He said, "Hell, no! Help me get these boxing gloves off. I know he can whip me now!"

Business Baseball Bat—MUTT

This one young guy and MUTT we were about the same age. He had the ability to do different things and we went into business a couple of times together, which was a drastic mistake looking back at it. When you're young and you're wild and crazy, you don't watch for snakes.

We went in the contracting business together. This was big-time business, I don't think he had any money and he lived with his mama. I think I might have had two or three hundred dollars, but we did have a little borrowing power. We had to buy the materials and pay for them. They wouldn't trust us to pay them, so we had to pay for a lot of materials to start with, so I had to put my money in the materials.

We got a pretty decent job and did real good. It was in the construction industry. We started on it and it went real good. We got half-way through and got a draw. I don't know if you know what a draw means or not, but they'll give you so much of your money for your equipment, and so much for the time you've got in. Of course, it's going to be less than what they owe you to make sure you come back. That's just business.

Now, we did real good until we got that draw. We got that draw, and I went to get him the next morning, and he wasn't there. I said, uh-oh." Guess what? I made about three stops and the third stop I found him. He was around there with, three women and they were having a blow-out.

But we had to go finish that job before we could get the rest of our money. Also, we didn't want to hold them up on the other work because we wanted to do another job for them. So, we had a couple of days that we could kind of kick back, and that's what we did. I just decided to stay there with them. That lasted about three days. Every time we ran out of booze, cigarettes or money, a woman would call her boyfriend and he would show up before long with her order. I never understood that. I just be damned if I would have done that. I would not have paid for my girlfriend to have sex with other men.

About the third day I said, "Man, we've got to get out of here." I was worried about the job. I went back to work, but I couldn't do anything by myself. I was hoping he'd have sense enough to leave. I went back and told him, "Man, we need to get to work." I noticed he had two big knots on his head.

He said, "I can't leave."

"What are you talking about?"

This woman there had two or three children and the youngest one was a boy. He said, "Every time I try to get up and leave, he hits me in the head with a baseball bat."

"What?"

He said, "Every time I get up to leave, he hits me in the head with a baseball bat."

The little boy said, "If you try to leave, I'm going to hit you in the head again."

He was enjoying it, and I don't think he really wanted to leave no how. He hung with them another day or two but that wound up being a week or two. I couldn't do anything at work, so I wound up having to get somebody else to come finish the job for us. I wound up losing money.

Money Worth Damn

Something hit me the other day. I was in Walmart and an attractive man and woman, probably my age, between 70 and 80, come walking down by and he was holding on to her arm. They were dressed good, and it looked like they had a good life, but they'd both gotten old. Getting older...it hit me...I've thought of it before, but that's one thing money can't buy is age. It doesn't make any difference what they have, they're going to soon be to the age they can't enjoy any of it.

EL TIGHTO—Career Woman

Well, I'm headed to my Sunday morning breakfast with two more of my associates, and these are real associates. They've got to where they started calling me at 6:30 a.m. in the morning. When he gets up, I don't believe he slows down. I think he starts putting on his clothes before he gets out of the bed. He's got the most energy of anybody I've ever seen in my life. Of course, it's paid off. He's been very successful. He's just a workaholic and he just can't be still. I've got to go this morning and discuss current events, and how his love life was this weekend, and all that. Well, that's the one who is 70 and just on the verge of getting married again. This will make him out six or seven marriages. I wish him luck.

One of my associates has been married several times. I think about five, six, seven times. I don't really know. He has made a fortune in business. He is talented at lots of things, but he just can't handle women. He married a career woman one time She had a real good job in an adjoining town. He was a contractor and he worked out of his home. He would go and spend the night with her. I don't know if they were going to move there or what. He stayed about a week and said that he was about to starve to death. When she'd come in from work, she'd bring some of that Chow Mein stuff in the cups, or some of that diet stuff off the salad bar or that kind of food. He said that he wasn't used to that. He was used to groceries. He worked real hard. He said she come in one evening and he said, "Darling, listen. I work real hard every day and I can't survive on this kind of food. What about tomorrow when I come in have me some rice and tomatoes and some white meat or some pork chops or something." He named off several items to her. Some cornbread. He said, "I would really love to have a chocolate cake."

He said that she didn't say anything. He went back over the next day and worked real hard. After work he took off. All the way thinking about what he was going to have for supper. He just imagined how good it was going to be. He said that he pulled to the front door and saw every one of his clothes on the front porch. He said that he just turned the truck around, backed up, loaded up his clothes and left. He said that he never did go back, and never has seen her again or heard from her again.

Coloring Book

I went to the doctor a while back. I have to take medicine since I'm getting older, and he examined me good. I hadn't been to a doctor in a good while. Anyway, he got through examining me and he said, "What sort of hobbies do you have?"

I said, "Well, I like to fish, and I like to read."

He said, "Well, that's not the right kind of activity."

I said, "What do you mean?"

He said, "You need to get you the simplest crossword puzzle you can find. If you can find a children's crossword puzzle or something similar. That's what you need to do to keep your mind active."

So, I went out the next Sunday morning at the bull session out there at the other place where I go with the two guys, and told them about it. Well, when I went back the next Sunday, they had me a nice coloring book and some color crayons. I'm talking about all colors. I mean, it was a good pack of crayons and a good coloring book. They gave me that and I sure appreciated it, but I wasn't having no real interest in it. I wound up giving it away up there at the library. I told them just to give it to one of those little young'uns that comes in there. But anyway, that thing rocked on a while. I come back in there another Sunday and they had another coloring book and told me that—you know, we was cutting up about it. They asked had I used up the other one and all that. So, they brought me another one in there and some more color crayons. It was a nice one, too, you know. Anyway, I took it and I got to looking at it. It said down at the bottom, on the sticker thing, that something was enclosed, and I said, "What in the world is that you reckon?" And I flipped that thing open and it had a bunch of those characters in there. You know, like Mickey Mouse and the lion and all that stuff. It had stickers. What you do you is, you pull the sticker off and put it on the picture. Well, there ain't but one problem. They didn't have the stickers labeled like one, two, three or like that, but then on the page it was on, you have to have the stickers on the page like one, two, three. It was all different sizes of stuff. I said, "My lord."

I peeled one of them off and I said, "Well, I'm going to see how this thing works." I went all the way through that coloring book and there was plenty of Mickey Mouses in there, but they were all the wrong size. I had to go through that coloring book twice and look on every page before I found the one that would fit correctly. What I'm saying is, I told them not to buy me no more like that because they were just too complicated for me.

King of the Castle—EL TIGHTO

Another time we went off fishing, and this same fellow that I told you was a workaholic. Well, he fished just like he worked. You just had to catch fish, just as many and as fast as you could. My friend had a place and we stayed up there about three days. We caught so many fish, instead of cleaning them, we'd take them to the fish market and let them clean them. We had three or four coolers of dressed fish. I was give plum out, but I just couldn't get him to quit

The night before, I was ready to go home, "Dumbo, you want to go home, don't you? I do. I've had enough of it."

He said, "Well, let's fish one more day."

That particular time, I was in his truck, so there wasn't much else I could do. We had pulled up in the canal where we were staying; it was real quiet. He said, "Shoot...would you go home if your wife called you and wanted you to come home?"

I said, "Yes, sir, I would go home."

He said, "I wouldn't. I wouldn't go home at all."

He was the king of the castle and all that. it wasn't two minutes later, we were idling up in there to anchor our boat off. We were through fishing for that day. It was dark. We started at daylight every morning and quit at dark every night. He liked to have killed me! The telephone rang and he turned the motor off. I could hear every word they were saying. It was his wife and she was just screaming in that telephone. I couldn't understand what she was saying, but she was making a bunch of racket.

He finally got through and he said, "Dumbo, she wants to talk to you."

Now, I liked her, so I said, "Okay, let me talk to her." A

"Aren't y'all in your boat?"

"Yeah. Why?" I said.

"You go back that truck in the water, and load that boat up, and bring his skinny tail home," She said. "I have answered this telephone till I am sick of it." She didn't say she missed him.

I said, "We can't. We've got three or four coolers full of fish at the fish market. It will be tomorrow before we can get the fish."

She said, "We don't need none of them fish. Just leave them right where they are. Let them sell them. You bring him home," She said and she hung up.

"Well, King of the Castle, how do you like that?"

He said, "Shoot! I still ain't going home."

So we didn't, and the next day I told him, "Now listen, I've had a damn bait of this."

We were in his boat instead of mine. It was one of them center console boats. I said, "At 12:01, I'm cranking up and we are gone."

He said, "What if we're catching fish?"

I said, "I don't give a damn if you're pulling one in."

Oh, and on top of that, let me throw this little tid bit in there. It was one of them Carolina Skiffs. This is no joke. On the front of that thing, where he was sitting with the trolling motor, he had taken PVC pipe and rigged it up and he had six different pole holders in front of him. It's a good idea if you like to troll fish. Well, it worked good for him, not for me, but for him. He had six poles and guess how many pole holders he had on the back? Zero! I weighed more than he did, so that put the back end of the boat sitting down deeper in the water. With no pole holders, I had to put my poles under my butt, and I couldn't fish but with one on both sides. He had six! Every time I'd lean one way or the other, the pole would come loose from under my butt and roll down to the back of the damn boat. And every time he'd catch a fish, he'd throw them back for me to put in the cooler. He was catching a lot more fish than I was because he was a lot better prepared than me. I'd had me a bait of all that, and it went on for three days.

On that last day I said, "12:01."

"What if we're..."

"I don't give a damn what you're catching. We're leaving at 12:01."

It came 12:01, and he was in the front of the boat not paying me any attention. I eased up and cranked the motor and put it in gear. "What are you doing?"

I said, "We're going home."

He said, "My Lord! We're catching fish."

I said, " What did I tell you? We are going to the damn house."

He pulled the trolling motor up and I took off. All of a sudden, the anchor rope slid off the side of the boat and went down in a bunch of stumps and nearly snatched us out of the boat at the same time.

But, we got the anchor loose and I brought his skinny ass home.

Fishing without Dumbo

Another one of my associates EL TITO. This is the one I was just talking about. He likes to fish. He's like being in a bed of piss ants, cause he can't be still. He wanted to go to the lake fishing. I told him I couldn't go that day. It was going to be the next day before I could go.

He asked me, "Is it all right if I take your boat and fish and you could come the next day?"

I said, "Well, yeah, that will be all right. You just go ahead and take it and when I start up there tomorrow, I'll just call you on my telephone, and find out what your 20-20 is and I'll meet you up there."

"Okay." So, he got my boat and took off.

The next day, I don't know what made me do it, but I think I called to see if he was catching any fish. I called and he didn't answer the phone. I waited 30 minutes and called him again and waited. I wasn't planning on going anyway until after lunch. I kept calling him, but he never would answer the phone. So, I finally called his wife and asked her if she'd heard anything out of him. She said, "No, he went off with (can't even call the guy's name) another friend of his. I guess. he went off with him fishing yesterday. I haven't heard anything from him."

"He did what?"

She said, "I haven't heard anything yet."

"They're in my boat!"

"What?"

I said, "Hell, they're in my boat. I can't get him to answer the telephone."

She said, "Well, I be dogged."

I called a few more times and never did get a hold of him.

He finally got back two or three days later, and I scorched his ears good. He never did come up with a good excuse for taking the other man. I don't know why he couldn't have waited on me that little length of time. Evidently, he wanted to go fishing with him worse than he wanted to go with me, but I wouldn't have cared if they've have used one of their boats instead of mine. Don't you agree?

Friends Rental EL CHEAPO

Today is Sunday and I've got a different crew that I meet with called friends. Well, let's don't call them friends. These are real associates. You'll find out over the years when you get to being 80 years old, you don't have friends, you have associates, because there's a thin line between money and friendship. Nobody ever needs to forget that.

These this morning I would call associates. One of these guys and I went to school together, and all these years he's been a small businessman, he's been very successful. He's a workaholic and he's greedy as hell. That's something else I'm glad I don't got. I'm not greedy and I'm not selfish. Of course, everybody wants to make money, but it's not the main importance to me. I hope we have a good morning.

We're headed up there, and we're going to have breakfast, and we'll sit around. The first thing we do is discuss current events. That's anything serious that's happened, or any news in our small town or in the world. Just like this mess over there in Syria, we'll probably have to discuss that this morning. We get all that off the table right to start with, and then we get on to my buddy.

My buddy has gotten a divorce at 70 years old. He was sitting around the house moping, and I finally talked him into going to the senior citizen's dance. He went twice, and he's had one just turn his head around, and it's just doing him the most good in the world. So, we'll have to hear all about the dance and all of that, and what she said. A lot of times, some of them old things that he did to me or I did to him will come up, and we'll leave there mad, but we'll make up. But just to show you about friends.

I've got a little bit of rental property and I've got a building the lease had come up on it. The people that had been there, had moved out of another building into that building. They have been with me a good long while, the lease come up, and his wife is a pretty shrewd operator, and she was trying to hold me down on the rent. I mentioned it to EL CHEAPO—don't ever do that. Keep your business to yourself. I went the next day to try to negotiate with them. He had already been with a set of plans and another lot to put them on. Now, that's my friend, mind you. My associate excuse me. We stayed mad about that about a year and wouldn't speak.

And one time before that, he had a big boat and he'd been taking me fishing. I had done some work for him. I said, "I'll tell you what let's do. Let's swap it out. You just take me fishing and we'll swap it out."

He said, "Okay."

Well, in about a month he sold the boat. So, he's left owing me money. I never said a word. One day he did a job for me that amounted to about the same amount of money he owed me. The first thing he did is—and I had a witness to the fact—he didn't even start good before he went up on me a couple of hundred dollars. That's just the way he operates. I like him, but the truth is the truth. I said, "Well, okay." What can I do?

When we got through and I went to pay him, I said, "Now, I'm going to deduct that money you owe me."

He said, "Money I owe you?"

"Yeah, you owe me the money that you were going to carry me fishing. You sold the dang boat and you suppose to took me one time."

"I don't feel like one time was worth what you owed me."

So, I wrote him a check for the difference. Boy, he blew, sculled and carried on, and we broke over that. I don't think it took, but about six months on that round.

But we've been on pretty good footing for the last three or four, five, six months, but it's about time for something to happen again. Don't do any business with your associates. Since then, we have completely broken up and I hate that. We had a lot in common, and I enjoyed him, and I think he enjoyed me, but you just could not trust him.

Let me add a little anecdote to that if that's what you call it. We've got a round table where several businessmen go in the mornings, and he mentioned to them that my lease was up on my building. Boy, you could see them men's ears just a flapping. The next day, I went to try to negotiate with my renter again and two of them had already tried to rent them a building. Don't ever discuss your business with your friends. Excuse me associates!

Gas

I went to the service station to get some gas in my boat. It's always my boat. It was one of them pumps where you have to pay ahead of time. I don't like them things. I always have to give them too much money, go pump my gas, and turn around and go back for my change. I'd already taken the gas cap off, in my behalf, trying to take up for me a little. It was a big boat, and it's got those big pole holders in the side of it you can put poles in. The pole holder was within three or four inches of the gas hole, or port hole or whatever you call it. I went to pay and come back. Guess what I did? I stuck the damn gas nozzle in the pole holder and put a gallon or two of gas in there. I'm lucky I had the plug out of the back of it, and I saw it running. If it hadn't had been for that, I'd have put about 20 gallons of gas inside my boat. What I was going to say is it ought to be against the law. They ought not to put a port hole so close to your gas thing because I know there's some more fools out there like me.

Glue in Nose

I have little things run across my mind once in a while, and I'm going to tell these in between some of these stories. This guy used to go out and drink at the clubs with us. One night he had a cold and he'd been out drinking, and he drank a lot. He went home and got him some of what he thought to be nasal spray to put in his nose. He squirted Elmer's glue up both sides of his nose. He wound up having to go to the hospital and get them to clean it out.

Green Stamp Bandit

Good morning! I'm up at 'em this morning, heading to the coffee shop. It's the highlight of my day.

I've just got a couple of little short stories I want to run by you here.

There was this guy from my home town, he was bad to steal and write bad checks, just anything under handed. They called this guy the Green Stamp Bandit. One time he went over to a small adjoining town and robbed a little store. He had the green stamps in his hand, this was back when they had green stamps. He stumbled and fell and hit his head on the edge of the counter. It knocked him out and that's where they found him. So, we just labeled him the Green Stamp Bandit.

Little Joe

This one is on a guy in my hometown and I'm going to call him Joe. They called him Little Joe. The first thing, he was tough. You know, like I said, all your little ones think they're tough. He was little, but he wasn't all that tough. I don't never remember him fighting nobody or nothing, but he just thought he was tough. He just really run his mouth.

He was down at the club one evening, sitting up there on the barstool and this guy came in. I knew him. He was a big guy and had big ol' hands. He walked over there and sat down by Little Joe. Little Joe said, "I advise you to get up and move."

He said, "Why, Joe?"

He said, "If you stay there, I'm liable to have to whip your ass. I'm a bad son-of-a-bitch."

The guy just reached over there, and I don't know how he did it, but it was just like a suction cup. He just put his hands on the top of Joe's head and squeezed and just picked him up off the chair. He said, "Joe, I'll tell you what you need to do. You need to get up and move because if you stay here, I'm liable to have to whip your ass."

Little Joe said, "Okay." He got up and moved!

Little Joe Bull Dog

Little Joe couldn't hold a job on account of his drinking, so once in a while he'd get out of a job and he'd come and want to work a little bit with me. I'd let him help me and just pay him for the day's work. This particular time, I had a little job to do out in the country out in a yard. We pulled up out there, and I went on around there tending to the job. Joe didn't come. I must have worked around there five or ten minutes and said, "Where is Little Joe?"

I went back around there, and he was still in the truck. I said, "Joe, get your ass out of there and help me."

He said, "I ain't getting out here."

I said, "What?"

He said, "I ain't getting out here."

I said, "Why?"

He said, "You see that blue eyed bulldog up there?"

I said, "What?"

"You see that blue eyed that bulldog up there?"

I looked on the porch and there was an old, fat bulldog laying on his back. He didn't look like to me he was no danger to nobody. I said, "Joe, that damn dog ain't going to bother you."

He said, "I ain't getting out here. I ain't messing with no blue-eyed bulldog."

I went back and finished the job by myself and carried him back to town and didn't give him a dime.

Keys in the Door

I carry three sets of keys with me in my truck. I've got two back there in my toolbox and one in the truck. That way if I lose one, I've got another one, and if I can't find that one, I've got another one. That's about the only way I've found that I can keep from locking myself out of my truck. I always leave my toolbox unlocked so I can be sure to get in.

I went to the coffee shop the other morning and come back out and I gave a guy some relish out of my truck. I opened up on the other side of my truck, which I usually don't, but the relish was on that side, and I gave him the relish. I was interested in that, talking about that. Well, I went back in the restaurant and when I got ready to leave, I went back out and did not have my keys. I said, "Well, I'll be damned. What did I do with my keys?" I couldn't find them, so I went around to the toolbox. I said, "This ain't no big deal. I've got another set over here in the toolbox. I'll just get them, and I'll run across those others directly."

So, I did. I got up town and went to stop for a red light and this woman hollered at me, "Mister, Mister!" I looked over at her and she was there at the edge of the road at the red light. I rolled my window down so I could hear what she wanted. She stuck my set of keys in the window to me. I said, "Bless your heart. Where did you find them?"

She said, "You left them in the door."

James Good

There were two brothers in my hometown, about the same age as me, and both of them would climb a tree to tell you a lie. Have you ever seen anybody like that? They'd rather tell you a lie than tell you the truth. Everybody knew how they was. They were both very likeable, and they were both big fishermen, and I knew them pretty well. It didn't make no difference if they didn't catch but two, when they got back it would be 99 or some God-awful number. One day they were at the drug store, where we used to gather and shoot the bull in the morning times. One of them was telling something and his brother said, "You lie! You lie! You lie!"

"You know you lie."

He said, "Look a-here."

He said, "I don't lie near as bad as you do!"

Sneakie Snake

Sneakie Snake was adjustable. I've got some many different things to tell about him, but I'm probably going to get them all mixed up. I am going to try to remember them as I can when they come along.

Sneakie could be in New York City working or in the highest, swankiest place in town, or in the ghetto. He could mix with the rich, he could mix with the poor, and he was just as happy anywhere you put him. He was fast on his feet. I reckon that's the reason they called him Sneakie.

I had a buddy; SNEAKIE SNAKE, well, we were buddies until a few years back. I don't know what happened. He's been sick, and having to use a walker, and breathing machine. He moved out of town before he got sick, and because of drinking and driving. He couldn't come to my house and I couldn't go to his. So, the last few years we've sort of grown apart. But I really enjoyed him, and I think he enjoyed me. We did some crazy, sorry things. A lot of them, I'm ashamed of, but some of them I would like to do again. I'm just going to tell you a little bit of the funny ones.

Junior and Sneakie Snake Back Scratch

SNEAKIE went to work at a plant where a lot of women worked and he loved the women. His other buddy wasn't working at the time. He rented an old doublewide trailer out of town, and he worked about two weeks and told his buddy, 'damned if he wasn't ready for a break.' He called in and told them he had had a heart attack. He loved to have them heart attacks. He told them that he wouldn't be back for a few days. He called two girls working out there and told them we were by ourselves in the woods. That afternoon about four o'clock they showed up. He and his other buddy were already drinking and having a good time. And those women stayed with them two or three hours and went home.

The next day about four o'clock the telephone rang, and this woman said, "Are you Junior?"

"I'm Junior."

"I hear you love sex."

"Well, I reckon I do."

"We'll be there in about 30 minutes."

"All right."

In about 30 minutes, they were there. They walked in the door and she said, "You must be Junior."

The old boy said, "I am."

She said, "Hit that bedroom."

"Okay," Junior said.

So, they did. That went on for a week and it was with different ones. They would tell some others. But they were out there partying and didn't give a damn. They were out in the woods and they'd come out. The story goes, I don't know whether they were married or not. I wouldn't tell you if I did. But, they'd come and sometimes they'd have one or two or three out there. Story goes that got to being a pretty good job, after a while. And I was told that were not all that good looking, but that really doesn't matter when you are drinking.

The last night Sneakie hung up with a pretty woman, but she was a big woman. She had a good figure, wasn't nothing wrong with her at all. And Junior hung up with one, well, she'd done been around a time or two. Well, those boys had a week of all this, and they felt terrible. They went to bed that night. They were staying in a mobile home, and beds were back-to-back in the bed rooms with no insulation in the walls. You could hear everything going on each other's room. They partied until they couldn't go no further. I don't know how to say this. I reckon I could say that they tended to their business. Junior could hear his buddy, and his buddy could hear him in there, and he was tending to his business.

Well, Junior rolled over and went to sleep. He'd had enough of that. Before he got to sleep, he heard his buddy in there a moaning and a groaning and carrying on. He woke up and said, "What in the world?" He said that he looked over there at the woman he was with and she was wide awake.

Junior said, "Well, I reckon if I don't get going here it's going to make me look bad."

So, they went at practiced again and rolled over to go to sleep. But his buddy was in there just moaning and Junior said, "Good God a mighty." Junior didn't want to be out done, so he practiced one more time.

When Junior got through and laid there, trying to sleep, and his buddy started again. "Good gracious a life. I can't handle this." So, story goes that Junior practiced again about a half a time and he just said, "To hell with it and finally gave up. He's just a better man than me."

The next morning Junior and his girlfriend for the night were the first ones to get up. These were top-notch women, some of them. She came in there with her panties and bra on, and Junior in his drawers. Her eyes were all sunk back in her head and her hair was all messed up. She just looked like she'd been through hell. She said, "I feel like hell."

"Well, you ought to. Hell, y'all stayed up all night."

She said, "We damn sure did."

Junior said, "Good God a mighty. I just can't hang with him at all."

She said, "What do you mean?"

Junior said, "Hell, I heard y'all in there. I tried to keep up, but I couldn't. I finally just gave up."

She said, "You mean you think we was practicing?"

Junior said, "Hell, I heard you in there."

She said, "That what you think?"

Junior said, "Yeah."

"Well, you're wrong," she said. "I scratched that little ol' SOB's back all night long."

I told you he was Sneakie. He always told me, if he didn't want to have sex he'd come up with an excuse. That particular night it was a scratched back. Old Junior liked to have killed himself, and that little joker wasn't doing nothing none of the time.

Sneakie Snake Ex-Wife

The next day, the last day, we had a party, a dinner party, and a cookout. There must have been 25 or 30 head there. Oh boy, we were boozing up and drinking. They got to where they just would bring beer and food and everything with them when they'd come. We were boogying down out there and having a good time. All of a sudden, this car come pulling up that driveway and Sneakie said, "Good God a mighty! There comes my ex-wife!"

I reckon she probably was hunting some child support money. I don't know what caused it, when he said that, everybody broke and ran. There were dog fennels out there. I don't know if you know what dog fennels are or not, but they were dried out and that makes it even worse. Everybody took off a running through them dog fennels. I got out there about 40 or 50 feet and I said, "What in the world am I running for? Hell, that ain't my wife." So, we all finally stopped and come back. But that broke up the party.

My buddy and I talked about it and added up and come to the decision that between the two of us we'd practiced with about 32 different women that week.

Sneakie Snake Jealousy

But the first thing I want to tell you is about jealousy. Jealousy is a terrible thing and I hope you don't have it. You've seen people if their neighbors get a new car or they build a new house, their so called friends can't hardly stand it. They've got to go buy them one. And I've had a touch of that, but over the years I've learned just to appreciate what I've got and be thankful, because by all rights,I shouldn't have anything. I was really headed down the wrong path.

This guy, we named him Sneakie Snake for good reason. He was a Sneakie snake! Whenever you hear these stories, you're going to realize how Sneakie he was. This is one on jealousy.

When we met, were both divorced and our minds were all mixed up. We drank and all that. This is kind of jumping the gun a little bit, but it just hit me, and I want to tell you this before I start.

He went in a little contracting business with a man, and about that same time I started a little business. But we began to do pretty good, by our standards. We were used to doing nothing, and we went a long time and didn't do anything hardly. We started doing better, and he and his girlfriend, and me and my girlfriend were real good friends. We'd get together on Friday nights. We'd party all that Friday night, and Saturday, and all day Sunday. Then we'd finally sober up and go to work on Monday.

Well, we would talk about our business, which I told you a while ago to keep your business to yourself, your friends are your enemies. I hate to say a word like that, but in a sense, they are because they're envious of you. I honestly think for the most part, they'd rather see you broke than they had to see you do good. As long as they're ahead of you, they're happy. You hear what I said? As long as they're ahead of you money-wise, they're happy. But if you get ahead of them, they don't like it. It's that plain ol' thing of jealousy.

Sneakie and I were to doing better and every Friday evening we'd get drunk, and both of our mouths would get to running. He'd wind up telling me what he made that week, and I'd wind up telling him. I could tell there was a sense of competition there.

One day, I rode through town and stopped at a red light. I remember it just like it was yesterday. I thought it was his girlfriend. She pulled up at the red light to my right in the prettiest pick-up truck I believe I have ever seen, even to this day. I thought it was her. The light changed. I drove through the light and I felt my face get just hot as fire. I looked up in the mirror and said, "What in the world is wrong with you?" And it hit me. It was one thing, plain and simple. It was jealousy. I said that I don't like this.

The next time we got together I said, "Listen, I want to tell you something." I told him the story. I told him about how I saw the truck and how jealous I got, and how we were talking money back and forth and looked like we were in competition.

He said, " I've got to tell you the truth. I feel just like you do."

"I'll tell you what. Let's do from here on out—let's not let money enter into our friendship."

He said, "You've got a damn good idea."

That kind of was like turning a light on with me. I said, "If we decide to go party or go fishing or whatever we do, you have your money and I'll have mine. Let's not get into the money."

He said, "You've got a deal."

We never got into the money thing again, and we stayed friends a long, long time. But I could tell as the years rolled on, his money got shorter and I did better. I've always thought that it had a lot to do with our friendship. We're still friends, I guess, but we don't 'associate' anymore. I always thought that had something to do with our friendship. I guess he got jealous without realizing it. I don't know. I hope not. But I don't wish him any ill will, and I wish we were going fishing this morning.

Sneakie Snake Job

I remember one time he needed a job. He was a carpenter. He went to Florida on some kind of a big job, building some big buildings, schools. He told them he had been a superintendent on some jobs, and damned if they didn't give him the top job. He didn't know a damn thing about it. He said that every time he needed to know anything, he'd just sneak out of there and go and ask some of them working, 'how do you do this' or 'how do you do that.' He wound up keeping that job until they got through with it.

He seemed to be able to adjust in most any situation. He was the slickest you'd ever seen. If he was with a woman and he was about half drunk and didn't want sex, he was good to have heart attacks, or bad to have heart attacks. He was about like Fred Sanford. If the need was necessary, he'd have a heart attack. Once in a while, he'd have a slight stroke, or he had leg cramps, just whatever the occasion called for.

I have known him when his wife got him in a pretty bad bind, and almost caught him doing something wrong. He'd get in bad shape, and they'd have to put him in the hospital. It's just whatever the situation called for.

I had a place out of town, and if it got hot enough, he'd go down there and stay a week or two until things kind of cooled off. He knew how to wiggle as good as I've ever seen in my life. He'd marry at the drop of a hat. He married one in another town one time and she was ugly. I mean, she was ugly, he said that he thought she had plenty of money. He stayed a little bit and found out right quick that she didn't have any. He didn't have a job. What in the world she wanted with him, I don't know. It wasn't working out, and she came home one evening and he was gone, and all of his clothes was gone. They were living in a mobile home with wheels and axles under it. He had sold the axles. They were probably worth a thousand dollars. Somebody came and bought them and he hauled ass.

Sometimes he would get drunk and run his mouth. He'd say so and so is a S.O.B and I don't care if you tell him. The next morning, early, he would call us and tell us to forget he said that.

He told me once about a nice looking married woman he went with and everything they did. He called early next morning and said to forget he said that. He said he was drinking and it was the old lying liquor. Sneakie would lie.

Sunken Boat

Me and my brother-in-law went down to the coast. I've done better just staying away from the coast. Seems like I've had a lot of trouble down in those big boats. We went fishing, and the first day we had a good time and caught a few fish. The next morning, we were going again, and I went up to the little store in the front, and the boats were in the water in the back. You stayed in the motel and you could leave your boats tied up in the water at night. Then in the morning you'd get in your boat and go.

My brother-in-law came in, and I was running my mouth. "Dumbo, come on, your boat is sinking." I didn't pay him any attention and just kept talking.

He said, "Dumbo, you better come on. The boat is sinking."

About the third time I said, "What did you say?"

"Your boat is sinking. I think it's sunk."

We took off and sure enough, it was sinking. And it was a nice boat. The back end was slam under the water, and the water was coming over the top of the transom, everything in there was floating. There was a guy standing there, and I got a feeling he was one of those Good Samaritans. It Is good that we've got people like that. He was standing there waiting on us with a pump and was going to throw it over in the boat to try to pump the water out so the boat would come up out of the water. It embarrassed me so bad until I told him we had it and we didn't need any help. I could tell he was disappointed, but he left.

I had to get over in the boat in the water. I don't know if you know anything about a center console boat, but that was about the most aggravating thing I've ever messed with. Anything you want to get under the center console you have to lay down in the boat and stick your head up under there. I had a little spare pump under the console, and I had to get down there and find it. I finally got it pumped out. Come to find out, I had live well aerators and we'd left it running and a pipe had broken. It was just pumping the water right into that boat. From beginning to end it, probably took us five or six hours to get the water out. Then we had to put the pipe back together. If we'd have gone ahead and let that guy pump the water out for us, we could have probably done it in an hour or an hour and a half. But whenever you're as dumb as I am, you don't do things like that.

Round Plug in a Square Hole

I had a nephew who really liked to drink. He wasn't completely right. I can't think of the word for it. All his screws weren't real tight. Good fellow. He'd find him a little penny ante' job for half a day. You'd think he was the owner or the manager. He went dressed clean cut and to look at him you'd think he was in charge, but he wasn't. He was just out there working. He claimed to have religion. He had a recording on his telephone. If you called his house, it would preach fire and brim stone to you, and you need to repent and get saved.

Once in a while he'd go off with Sneakie. Sneakie would take him off fishing, and he really liked to drink. He'd let him do the driving because he wasn't drinking. Sometimes he'd tell Sneakie, "I hate to tell you this, but the devil has took over and I'm just going to have to help you drink some of that beer." He would fill up, he'd go back home, and he'd get religion back. He'd get his recorder back on the telephone and repent.

Once in a while, I don't know whether it was therapy or what, but they were trying to help him. He said, "The first thing they do is, they give me them round plugs to put in them round holes. They didn't know it, I had better sense than that. There ain't no way in the world I was going to put them in the right hole. Then they give me a baby doll with the head off, and they gave me the head and told me to put the head back on the baby doll. Uncle John, I tried to stick that baby doll head up that baby's ass because I ain't wanting them to cut my check off."

On those pegs, they had both sides of them. They had the round holes and the square holes. And he knew which hole they went in, but he said that he wasn't about to put one of them in there. He said that he didn't want to lose his check!

Florida Fishing Tide Going Out

I'm just going to throw another one in about fishing and boating. I've always liked to fish and never have been good at it. I just enjoy it. When I was a little younger, I used to enjoy the drinking. We had some good times and some bad times. This particular time me and my Sneakie went to Florida fishing.

I had a big boat, or I say a big boat. It was about 18 feet long. We were fishing the flats. I had looked at the tide chart to be sure what they were going to be. We weren't catching any fish. I forget what time it was but they said that the tides was going to be low at a certain time. So I told Sneakie, "See that oyster bar right yonder?" They were out of the water. "Why don't we just anchor up right over there and the tide will be coming up."

About 30 minutes later, he said, "Dumbo, you see those birds walking on the water?"

"What?"

He said, "Do you see them birds walking on the water?"

I looked, and sure enough there was birds walking all in front of us.

"What about it? "

"That means that's the bottom."

"What?"

"That means that's the bottom. The tide is going out."

I said, "No, no, the tide is coming in. They had it on the bulletin board. They do it every day and it tells what time."

"Well, I don't give a damn what the thing said. The tide is going out."

It can't be! In a little bit, I looked back, and determined he was right. We were bogged down. It was so shallow, and we had a big motor on the boat, and we couldn't leave. We were just going to be stuck there for three or four hours. As luck will have it, we had a case of beer and we hadn't started drinking yet that day. We were serious fishing first thing that morning. We about as well just drink beer while this tide is changing.

We started in on the beer and sat there and talked and laughed and cut up, telling all these old crazy things I'm talking about now. And directly, the boat just fell over on one side. Well, it didn't fall all the way over, it leaned to one side. It was all the way down in the sand. We knew we was going to have to sit there a while. We got to noticing the boats of people out there fishing. They'd try to rescue us. They'd get off and watch us. I reckon they was looking for us to throw out a red flag or a white flag or a t-shirt or something and let them know if we were in disaster. Everybody on the water is like that. I've found the biggest percentage of your fishermen are good people. They're just as friendly and nice as they can be, and they'll help you. I guess in turn you'll help them because next time it could be you. If you've ever done much fishing, you'll find out there's no way to be totally prepared.

Then a little bit later a helicopter went to flying around over us, with a loudspeaker. We couldn't understand what he was saying. I reckon that was shore patrol. We didn't pay them no attention. We were just sitting there drinking beer. Directly my buddy said "I wish the hell they'd go on an leave us alone. Can't they tell we're having a good time."

"They can't get us for drinking and driving. I ain't even sure they can get us for public drunk. I wish he'd just go on and leave us alone."

Sneakie Willacoochee

Me and my old buddy, Sneakie, and our wives was heading out of town to a dance. We got a good early start so we could be there in plenty of time. We come through a little town and there was a boat sitting beside the road. We were in one of them big luxury cars. He liked those luxury cars. The big long cars, with the big wheels on them and electric windows. It had all those extras on it. Boy, if he could get behind one of them, he thought he was doing something. In fact, his wife said that she would live in a shack that she could see through the cracks in the walls in order to drive a new automobile.

We pulled up and he saw a boat. He said, "Turn around."

"What?"

They all called him 'baby'. He had blonde hair and they were just continuously combing it. The man came out and we looked at the boat and went back over to the car.

"Pay the man."

I forget how much it was now, $600 or something.

"Baby, we don't need that boat. You've already got four."

He was about like me. He's got too many to start with. " It don't make a damn whether I need the boat or not. I want the boat. Pay the man for the boat."

"Well, Baby, when I give this man this $600, we aren't going to have but two or three hundred dollars left."

He said, "Don't worry about that. I'll make some more money."

Treasure Hill President

The next one I'm going to tell is on me and Sneakie. We really pulled some doozies, back in our day and this is just one of them.

There was a big crowd that always get together at somebody's place and drank and carried on. People that party can find each other. We'd have a bunch of ol' trashy women with us, and have what we thought, was a good time. Looking back at it now, I got a lot of misery out of it, but we thought we were having a big time.

We was drinking and boogying down, and we stayed two, three or four days at this placed named Treasure Hill. Jenie Benie had some mobile homes up on a hill that he rented out that were kind of a low-income type of deal. It was isolated from everywhere and that was just a good drinking spot. We'd been out there several days with them women and some more. There were probably eight or ten of us, somewhere in that range. We'd been drinking and the guy that owned the place—we called him Jeenie Beenie—he would get drunk, drunk. He'd get so drunk till once in a while he'd just pass out. He'd say, "SOB," and just throw his head on the kitchen table. He was liable to be out two or three hours, then he'd wake up and go again.

When you get drunk you get real intelligent, or I always did. We got to talking about politics and somebody mentioned calling the White House. "Well, let's do that." I know you think this is a lie, but it ain't. We called the White House and got all the way through to this lady.

I'm don't remember her name and would not tell you if I did, but she said that the president was out of the country and wouldn't be back and asked could she help us. I said, "Yes, ma'am, you can." I started rattling off about how I didn't like this and that.

That girl I had with me said, "Let me talk with that…"

"Just a minute." She snatched that phone out of my hand and she went to cussing and a ripping and a raring to that woman.

The lady said, "I'm not used to this kind profanity and I don't have to listen to it." She hung up.

Oh, boy, that was funny to us! Oh, we laughed and carried on. we were rocking and rolling.

It was around dinner time. That was back before they had all these cell phones. We had our poker games up there. We heard something hit the gravel. It was just an ol' hard clay hill and when a car turned in there, you could hear the tires on that gravel. There was a black limousine coming up the hill. It looked like it was as long as a school bus, and it had long antennas all over it. You talk about scattering. Me and my girlfriend hid under the bed, some went out the back door, I don't know where the rest of them went. Jenie Benie was sitting in the kitchen with his head on the table. If you've ever been to a good party like that, they'll be stuff scattered everywhere. We had beer cans everywhere, and mixed drinks, liquor, etc., and he was the only one left in the trailer. It was quite as a church mouse. They knocked on the door. He didn't answer. He'd passed out drunk with his head on the kitchen table. We heard that door creek open and they called him, "Are you Mr. So-and-so?"

"Yeah, "Who are you SOBs?"

"This is the CIA or the Secret Service or whatever."

"What?"

Boy, you talk about sobering up! We could hear him. He said, "Yes, sir, Your Honor. What can I do for you?" He got sober in a hurry. "We've been informed that there have been obscene phone calls from this phone going to the White House. Now, we can look here and tell what's going on. So, we're going to tell you what we're going to do. If you'll just cease and desist right now, we'll go on and leave you alone, but if we get another phone call, you're all going to jail."

Genie Beanie said, "You're damn right, Your Honor. We're going to cease and desist right now. Just as quick as I can get these SOBs out of here, we're going to cease and desist."

We heard them leave going down the hill. He said, "You bunch of SOBs come out here!" We all went back in the living room. Back then they didn't have these cell phones. They had telephones with cords. He just snatched that son-of-a-gun out of the wall. He said, "You sons of bitches, go home now, and I mean now! And don't never come back!"

Treasure Hill Poker Room MUTT

Genie Benie and Sneakie were building a poker house. They finally got through and we started playing poker. He charged for playing poker by cutting the pot. Of course, it didn't do him any good because he'd get drunk and loose his money and the pot money. I remember one particular time, my buddy MUTT had a girlfriend, and she worked and he didn't. Well, he worked some, but not much. One night in particular, he was playing and he asked her if she had any money and she said, "No, I told you I don't have any money."

He kept on and she finally turned her pocketbook over and poured the money out. He got him enough to put in the last pot. Naturally, he lost that hand and they went home broke.

Treasure Hill Poker Room MUTT 2

Another time, MUTT—the one with the fly rod, was playing poker, and naturally, he was drunk, and he'd lost. I don't know how much, but a hundred dollars or more. He finally got a good hand. He had four queens or four aces or something and we were playing seven-card stud. Boy, he hooped and hollered and laughed and carried on and he showed everybody. Well, he didn't show his cards to the ones that were in the hand, but he showed them to everybody else. You know how you've always got your onlookers. I don't like that because they can see your cards, and if they're with somebody, they can motion for them to turn over. They were raising every card and he could have gotten him a big pot, but I think he wound up winning about $10.

Treasure Hill Poker Room—Genie

Well, I'm going to go on with a little story about the same two buddies that built the poker house out there. Anyway, if he ever had any money, and he usually lost the pot and lost the cut money, he'd get drunk. But if he ever got ahead any bit, he had a freezer out there and he'd put his money. He'd hide it in that freezer. Well, his buddy knew it, the one that helped him build the gambling room, he knew it. We got to having a good one week. Every time you'd turn around, we'd sneak out there and get in that jar and get us $20. Then we'd be back before you know, it for another $20. We kept on until we got every bit of his money out of that jar. But you know, Genie never mentioned it to us. He must have been drunk and forgot where he put it.

Treasure Hill Poker Room 4

The next time, my buddy was staying up there with him a little bit, and they were building a poker room. They gambled, you know, and he was building a poker room. He would cut the pot, and he was going to make money off the poker game. So, they just plum quit drinking to work on that poker room. I mean, they built a good building sure enough. They worked on that thing about two weeks. Me and my buddy, we had us a little ol' job, we'd go over there. On Saturday would come and we'd come over there drinking and raising sand, and we'd aggravate them about when was they going to drink a beer or was they ever going to drink another beer.

Anyway, we went in one evening and he called. They had them nail aprons on and was measuring everything and a-sawing. One of them was a good carpenter, my buddy was; he was a good carpenter. Well, he called them out there and said, "Let's show these SOBs how to get drunk." By George, they did. I mean to tell you, they tore loose and got with the party. We wound up out at the, I believe it was, the VFW out there.

He went through town, and he was crazy when they got drunk, this other fellow was, and shot several of the windows out. I don't know what all he did, but that was some crazy doings.

Sneakie Snake Out of Money

Sneakie, got his income tax check back. He was working at that time. It was between seven and eight hundred dollars. I had some money. I didn't have a bunch. I hadn't got mine yet.

We took our girlfriends and hauled buddy to a close town where they had a real good band. A lot of people went to it. Boy, we danced and boogied down and had a big time. Sneakie has never cared anything about money. By that, I mean he likes money, but he loves to spend it. We got over there and were dancing. That was back whenever them hot pants had just come out. The waitress came over and I have to admit, she did have pretty legs. He started tipping her, and I know I seen him tip her $20 a time or two. Probably before it was over, he started tipping her more than that. He said to her, "Honey, just keep them coming."

We were drinking them mixed drinks, them high-priced drinks and the women were. We had so many drinks on that table before the night was over till you couldn't put your elbows down. That's how many drinks we bought. We got that many ahead is what I'm trying to say. Boy, I mean, he was laying with that woman. Well, naturally, before the dance was over, he went over there somewhere on the other side and told somebody that I wanted to whip their ass. Well, I didn't know it. I was dancing and noticed young people crowding up around me. Not the women, the men. They were getting closer to me on the dance floor.

Finally, I said, "Sneakie!"

Boy, he was boogying down, just watching. "Sneakie, what in the hell is going on?"

"I'm afraid they want to whip your ass."

I said, "For what?"

He said, "Because you said you wanted to whip their ass."

"That's horse manure. I ain't said a damn word to them men."

I finally stopped right in the middle of my dance and said, "Listen, I don't know what the son-of-a-bitch has told y'all, but I ain't said nare word about whipping none of you. I came in here to have a good time and I want to have a good time. I like all of y'all."

I stuck my hand out and they shook hands with me, and we went back to dancing. We left there drunk, naturally, and spent the night at a motel.

I got up the next morning to go eat breakfast and walked out of my room ahead of him. He came walking out there right quick. I knew he was waiting. He said, "Hey, you got any money?"

"I got a little bit, but I don't have much. Why? Wait a minute. Why in the hell do you need money?"

He said, "Dumbo, I spent every damn penny I had in that bar last night."

"You mean to tell me..."

He said, "Hell, yeah. I bought them drinks, and then tipped that woman, and I don't think I've got but $5 left, and we've got to have breakfast."

I had to loan him five or ten dollars or something where we could go eat breakfast. But that's just the way he loved it.

Sneakie & MUTT

Sneakie, and our other little buddy MUTT—the one that liked the boats—went across the river. Like I told you, they loved to get across that river. Just something about that water that they just couldn't stand. If you cross that water, you just had to get drunk. There was a club or two up there so they could drink and show out. That's where they'd always wind up. It was a Friday evening, and it got right busy. They wound up latching on to two women. it rocked on a while and the women decided to let them go home with them. So, they went out in the boondocks to a mobile home right up against the edge of a swamp. They got to partying down and having a good time, and I don't know what all went on, but I've got an idea.

Sneakie was on the commode, and I don't know what MUTT was doing, it had gotten dark by then. All of a sudden, there was some lights come turning in there and the woman said, "Oh, my Lord! That's my husband. Y'all got to get out of here."

Boys, they took off out the back door. Sneakie still didn't have his britches all the way up. They hid in the edge of that swamp. It was rough sure enough. If you've ever been in a South Georgia swamp, you know it was rough.

About that time her husband said, "We're just going to kill the SOBs."

The only smart thing they done in the whole deal was MUTT had his truck keys in his pocket. That guy said, "Where are they? We're going to kill the SOBs."

He said that they didn't go far but they said that they just got to running back through that swamp and got deeper and deeper in mud and water and getting scratched all over. About that time, they went to shooting at them. They went to hiding behind them logs and stumps. That went on for about 30 minutes. It quieted down and he heard an automobile leave. They were probably drinking too, and they were going back to the club to get them some more beer I imagine.

They sneaked back up there and they hadn't bothered their truck, so they cranked it up and started coming back home. Sneakie said, "Man, we can't go across that river bridge. I bet you, they're waiting on us right now." That was the way you had to go to get back home. "We go across that damn bridge. They're going to be there waiting on us. Hell, they'll kill us."

So, they decided on another route. It was about 50 or 60 miles out of the way. They run out of gas, naturally, and had to hitchhike home. Sneakie said he didn't know whether it was worth all that or not.

Sneakie and Dumbo Road Trip

One day we ran into these two girls, or women, they were very attractive. One of them had a boyfriend that had taken a job out of state and he had to go back to work, but he didn't have the money to get him there. As soon as he got there, he could pick up his paycheck, and he would pay us for the gas and everything we spent going up there. The two girls, well, they were a little on the trashy side, I guess you'd say. I found out one thing. I found this out on another deal, but it applies to this one sure enough. If anybody tells you they've got the money look at it. I said to Sneakie, "I ain't got any money."

SNEAKIE said, "Don't worry about the damn money. I've got plenty of money."

"All right. If you've got the money, we'll go."

We were anticipating getting him up there and getting rid of him, then we were going to go boogie down. We thought we might just spend the night since it was so far. We were going to be drunk, and not be able to drive and hung over and all that.

We took off. We weren't far down the road when we had to start buying hamburgers and all that kind of stuff. Then we had to buy some pantyhose, and this and that. They had on their high heel shoes and their dresses. They were all dolled up and, boy, we were liking that. One of them, said that her dress just didn't match her shoes. Sneakie had to buy her a dress.

We were boogying down and having a good time Finally, me and Sneakie and his girlfriend had to get in the front seat, and the man and his girlfriend was in the back seat. They had a sheet, and I don't know what was going on, but they put the sheet across them. That was the one I was supposed to be going to court. That really made me feel good. When you're drinking it don't bother you, and we'd done started drinking a little bit.

We finally got to his job. It was a big company and it was all behind a chain-link fence and they had a guard shack. He walked up to the gate and the guy let him in. Well, he'll get his check right quick and we'll go cash it and then we'll be rid of him. Then we can go party down. He stepped back out the gate and told us, "Go ahead, I can handle it from here.'"

And Sneakie said, "Hold on just a damn minute. You can handle it from here all right but let's go cash that check."

"I have got it now." He went back inside that chain-link fence and they locked the gate behind him.

Well, that wound that up, that Sneakie had done spent all of his money, and I'd spent the little bit I had. Or I say all of his money. He said that he had a pocket full, so I wasn't really worried. We left there. We had started drinking pretty good. The girls wanted another hamburger and Sneakie ordered a big 7-Up and I said to myself, "What in the hell does he want a big 7-Up and him drinking beer?" When the girl come back (they wore them hot pants at them drive-ins) he asked her how much it was. She told him and he throwed another dollar up there and he reached in his pocket and he said, "Dumbo, that's every damn dime I've got. You got any money?"

"What? I told you I didn't have any money to start with and I've done spent all of mine."

"Well, that's a hell of a note." He reached in the glove compartment and he had a pint of liquor. I believe it was Ole Crow or something like that. He had that 7-UP so we started on 7-UP and Old Crow. We couldn't do anything then but turn around and go home since we didn't have any party money. We hadn't even danced with the women kissed them or nothing.

So we boogied on down back the road headed home. Well, they got hungry again. They went in their pockets and got enough money to buy some Coca-Colas and crackers. There's two things we forgot. The first thing is we got back to the toll bridge and it was 75-cents. I remember that just like it was yesterday. Seventy-five-cents and we didn't have the damn money to get across the toll bridge!

One of the girls had on them party dresses. It was in the middle of nowhere and was hilly where we were. I pulled up to the toll booth. It was about twelve or one o'clock at night. It was back when the black people had the afros. I'd been working with some at my job, and I thought I could talk cool, so I figured I could get us on through there since no one was there but him.

We had that music rocking and I said, "Hey, Man, we ain't got 75-cents. How about letting us slide on through here?"

He said, "Hey Man, you slide back up their side of that road until you come up with 75-cents."

What were we going to do then? We backed up beside the road and I said, " if we sit here very long, he'll call the damn law. We're drunk, and he could tell it." And we were showing out sure enough.

About that time, we heard a car coming. It was dark and at night out in the middle of nowhere, we heard it a long way down the road. One of them girls said, "When that car starts getting up close, y'all lay down in the seat."

That car topped that last hill and she said, "Lay down."

So, we laid down in the seat. That car come a rocking down the road and went to slowing down. She stepped out in the first lane and pulled that dress up good and high and they hit their brakes. The guy gives her a dollar and we got across the toll bridge.

The other thing we forgot was to put money back for gas. We got on down the road a little way and we wasn't paying the gas tank any attention. All of a sudden Sneakie said, "Dumbo, we're about to run out of gas."

"What? I thought you had gas."

He said, "Hell, this thing don't get good gas mileage. We've done filled up two or three times."

It was one of them Chrysler New Yorkers, one of them, what he called—a luxury car. It had everything in it. It was an old car. We got to worrying about gas and we pulled over on the side of the road and had them girls go through their pocketbooks. We come up with a dollar. We got back on the road and it was about two o'clock in the morning, and we come to this service station in the forks of the road out in the middle of nowhere. The lights was on and two men were standing out there by the gas pumps. That was back when gas was cheaper than it is now. We pulled up there and was just a boogying down and hollering and laughing, cutting up and told them we wanted a dollar's worth of gas.

We sat there and talked a few minutes, laughing and cutting up. It was in the summertime. We rolled the window back down and handed the man a dollar and said, "Thank you." We cut out on down the road. We didn't go ten miles before we run out of gas. What I figured out. I don't believe the service station was even open. I believe that light was on out front by that pump, I reckon for vandalism. And them men didn't even work there. They were just standing out there talking, and us being idiots like we were, and drunk too, we just gave them our dollar and drove on off. Boy, I bet they said, "Well, them's some dumb son-of-a-bitches, ain't they?"

We ran out of gas, and it just so happened there was a house up the hill and we could see a light on up there. The girls told us, "Listen, if we start back down here in an automobile, (Oh, they had blankets and all that stuff) y'all take them blankets, and lay down in the back seat. Put the blankets over the top of you."

In a little bit we heard an old truck come rattling down the hill. We got up under those blankets. We could hear them talking, and he put gas in the car, and left. We cranked up and headed on towards home. We didn't get down the road ten miles before we run out of gas. That bastard had put just enough gas in that thing to get us away from there. There was a lot of hills up And a lot of them—what you call them things a side of the road—them steel things, them barriers or barristers, to keep you from running off down the hill. I was just a hitting them things. Click, click, click down through there. And Sneakie had a heart attack. I said, "Sneakie, you just as well get back up. I know there ain't a damn thing wrong with you, you, ain't had no heart attack."

I was all over the damn road about ten miles down the road. It was probably a good thing because I would have probably run off one of them damn hills before it was over—we run out of gas again. By this time, we had drunk that pint of liquor and were beginning to feel bad and get sleepy. It must have been two or three or four o'clock in the morning. Sneakie said, "The hell with it. I'm going to bed." He just passed out in the back seat.

I said, "Well, I've had it, too." I just slumped over in that gal's lap. Now, bear in mind, we hadn't even kissed them. We just said 'the hell with it.' We'd gone as far as we could go. About daylight something woke me up. I looked up and them girls was heading towards home, down the middle of that road with them high heeled shoes on, just a getting it. I just laid back down in the seat. Sneakie did too. We'd had it!

I believe we'd have slept all day right there if the law hadn't got us. Sometime later on, I heard a noise and it woke me up. It was them women. They had been all the way home. I don't know how much further it was to the house. But probably, if somebody had passed by them, they'd probably pull them skirts up and they'd hitchhiked and got them a ride. They had borrowed somebody's car and come all the way back and brought us some gas. We got back home! HALLELUJAH! That was one hell of a trip.

Sneakie lied and he didn't have all that much money. We didn't even get a kiss! We ran out of gas two or three times. I told Sneakie if I ever went off with him again, I was going to see the damn money before I left home.

Watch Stop

I'll tell one now here that's a little bit ironic. One of these associates that I eat with on Sunday is an ex-state patrolman, a GBI man and the other was an ex-sheriff. They went out to a flea market. Bear in mind, this guy has seen a lot of cases, and seen a lot of crooked things so, he ought to be pretty well on the ball. They had the prettiest jewelry there he had ever seen. He said that they had a watch. They wanted four or five hundred dollars for it, and it was a name brand sure enough. He chewed them down to $50. He had a friend that was tighter than he was. He was an ex-sheriff and he bought one, too. He gave it to his wife, and she was tickled to death. It was pretty sure enough. So, she wore it to work. She worked around a bunch of people, and in about three days, it quit running. She didn't know where he got it. He didn't tell her the whole story. She carried it by a jewelry store to see what was wrong with it; it being such a good watch. The jeweler told her it was made out of plastic. She gave him hell! The embarrassment of showing that thing off everywhere and then finding out it's made out of plastic. If you've ever had to deal with any women or you've ever been married, you can know he had a few bad days.

Danny's Bidet

We're talking about November the 6th, 2013. We're past Stargate 6 and I've just purchased a bidet. Yes, an 8-6100-WT-series bidet, which is one notch above Sammie's bidet. And it's got all the options of front and back. It'll warm the water up to whatever temperature you want. It's got a massage feature and it's got a blow dry feature. One thing I've found out this morning, you've got to be located within two inches of a spot on that seat or it won't work. I just wanted to let you know that I fully recommend this thing. If it tears up, I'll have one in stock. I'm thinking about getting one to carry with me on the truck. I got the wide tail series, the WT-series, and I would recommend that to anybody. I've done and tested and wiped and I'm totally clean. I would have probably wiped my face with it after, but I probably wouldn't have told nobody. Its two sizes bigger than Sammie's and has more options.

Hurt My Back

I could tell several stories on this guy, (GUY's what I call him here) but I am only going to tell a few, and I think you will get the point.

I think he must have drawn a crazy check because I never knew of him working a full-time job anywhere. Once in a while, he would come and work for me. But he was not too crazy to play Bingo in different towns almost every night. He would go to the Church, they would give money and food to him, his wife and child. Then they would go to Bingo game. I had a businessman tell me one morning that he really felt good cause a man had come by, he did not have any gas in his car or money for food and had to take his child to a doctor in another town. He said that he gave him money plus a tank a gas. He said that it really made him feel good to help someone like that. I told him that was wonderful! Then I told him the story that you need to be careful; not everyone is honest. I asked him what the guy looked like and if he knew his name. it just happened to be the person I was talking about. He said, "Well, I will be damned." He came back later and my secretary gave him twenty dollars.

He owed me money from working for me. He came walking by my house one day. He had tears in his eyes and said that he knew he owed me, but could not pay me but he wanted twenty dollars. He went on to say that he was not going to pay that back either because he was dying with cancer within a short time. I told him no. I saw him about three years later and he was fat as a pig.

Later on, a man hired him to pick up eggs at an egg farm. He was going to have to set him up a mobile home and get him a septic tank. It was going to take him a while so he put him in a motel for a couple of weeks until he could get the mobile home set up. He said that every time he'd turn around, the baby was out of diapers, or he had to have this and that and the other. He said that he done had a good bit of money in him, plus the aggravation, before he ever got the mobile home set up. He finally got it set up, and this guy went to work. He worked real good. He went with him that first day to be sure he knew what he was doing and he was pleased. "Man, I got me a good man here."

So, the next morning he didn't get in a real big hurry to get there. He had something else that he needed to do. He went later on and there was nobody at the houses. He went back to their place and knocked on the door and the man's wife come to the door. Where is your husband?"

She said, "He's in the bed. He's sick."

"Can I talk to him?"

"Yeah, just go on back there."

He said that he walked back in the bedroom and he was laid up in the bed. "What in the world is wrong with you?"

"I hurt my back yesterday and my lawyer told me not to move until I met with a doctor and find out just exactly what's wrong with me."

"Say that again."

"I hurt my back yesterday and my lawyer has told me not to do anything until I talk to the doctor and find out exactly what's wrong with me."

This fellow said he didn't know what to do or say, so he just turned around and left.

This fellow that owned the chicken houses, well, I've heard stories about him all my life. Heard that when he was young, he was tough, and he loved to fight. They say he and some others went to the University of Georgia to a hot dog stand, and there were some people from different towns, and this fellow wanted to fight. He said, "Yeah, we'll fight."

They went outside and he said "Where do ya'll want to go?"

"Well, we're going to go to so-and-so's."

He said, "All right. I'll tell you what I'll do. I'll just leave my car here and I'll ride with you." For some reason they decided they didn't want to go.

This same fellow had to survey some land adjoining a big man's land that carried a gun. His daddy had bought him a farm here just to get rid of him cause he was a nut. He started working and wasn't long before the big man showed up. "What in the hell are you doing out here! I`ll shoot you right now. Get off my land."

Surveyor said, "Before I start, we might as well settle this." He started taking off his jacket.

The other man laughed and said, "Go ahead." Surveyor never had any more trouble with him.

Getting back to the story, this same fellow is the fellow that owned the chicken houses. He left and stayed gone about an hour and rode around. He was looking at the pros and cons, about the lawyer and the suing and sending him to the doctor, and this and that and the other. He said that he thought about it, and he went back and knocked on the door. The wife opened the door and he went on back there where he was laid up in the bed. He said, "I got to thinking about this thing. I've been mighty good to you, but I'll tell you what I'm going to do. It's three o'clock right now. I'm going to give you 30 minutes to get everything you've got out of this house, or I'm going to come back in 30 minutes and I'm going to whip your ass. I just promise you I'm going to do it every day. At three o'clock you can look for me. I'll be here and I'm going to whip your ass until you do move." (His brother is the one that told this on him.) He said that he come back in about 30 minutes and they were just throwing stuff out of that front door. He left and stayed gone about another 30 minutes and when he came back, they were gone. They were gone and all of the furniture was gone and that was the end of that story.

Mi Ti Lounge

Working down at a beach one time, I got off one afternoon and went down to a lounge. It was called the Mi Ti Lounge I believe. And I was single back then. I walked in the front door. A guy in there stood up and waved at me to come. He whispered "Man, I've got three women over here. There ain't but one of me. You need to come sit with us."

I said, "Okay." I sat down.

He whispered to me right quick that he was about out of money and would I loan him some money. He was going to pay me back next week. You know how that goes. I didn't even hardly know him, but I let him have it. I was crazy, but we stayed there until they closed the Mi Ti Lounge down. Then everybody wanted to go eat something.

We went up the beach there to a place—the name of it was Strickland's—and it was a real nice restaurant. We went in and were waiting for the waitress, and I kind of glanced up under the table and I saw the girl I was with rubbing one of the other men's legs. Something said," Hello!"

In a little bit the waitress came and we gave her the order. Oh, they ordered lobster tail and filet mignon and I don't know what all kind of stuff. I was the one that was going to be paying the bill. About that time, I saw that woman, my girlfriend supposedly with, rubbing the other man's leg again. I got to figuring up in my mind what that was going to cost me, and seemed like back then it started off about $20 or $25 a plate. I got to figuring it. Luckily, I had enough money in my pocket to pay it. I got up and went to the bathroom to kind of gather my thoughts. I looked and there was an exit door right beside the bathroom. I figured it was locked. I pushed the door and it opened. I stepped out the door going wide open. I run like the hundred-yard dash! I don't believe the record holder could have out run me. I ran about four or five blocks up the beach to my car, and got in it and went home.

The next day that guy come in the store and said, "Where did you go to last night?

"Man, I saw that damn woman wasn't going to be with me, and I'd spent all that money up at the lounge, and I had to buy all that high-priced food! Shit, I got out of there!"

He said, "Well, I'll tell you what happened. We couldn't pay the bill, they made the women turn their pocketbooks upside down and made us turn our pockets out, and we still didn't have enough money. You're barred from Strickland's for life."

I said, "Well, that suits me just fine." From then on, and I worked down there for a year or two, every time I'd pass Strickland's—I was young back then—

I'd duck my head down so they couldn't see me. I thought that they was going to try to put me in jail. But I learned one thing out of that. When you're off with a bunch like that drinking and carrying on, watch what's going on around the table.

DUMBO—Christmas

Well, I did my Christmas shopping yesterday. That was a real pleasure. I use the front seat of my truck for my office and it stays scattered all the time. There's always napkins all over it, there's a payment book or two and this and that. I'm not neat and tidy like a lot of people. Of course, I don't want to be as neat and tidy as some people I know, but I'd love to be about halfway in between.

I had a variety of different things to do. I don't try to pick out presents, so I went to a restaurant and got gift cards By the way, if you buy a hundred dollars' worth, they'll give you twenty dollars' worth of free tickets. Then I had to go to Belk's and get some of their gift cards. Then I had to go to the dollar store and get some of them cheap Christmas cards. I had to carry my address book with me with all the different addresses. I had a half a dozen of those things to send off. After all of that, I had to go to the bank. There's one or two of them I send cash money. I put the cashier's check in an envelope with the Christmas card. I am scared to send money because you can lose it.

The very first thing I do after I get all that together is to address every one of them Christmas cards in the front seat of my truck, I've got to look them all up in the address book. I wish you could see it. I bought it fifty years ago when I started in business. I have every one of my old customers in it plus my family,and they have begot and their children have begot. I think they take after me, and most of them have moved a time or two. A lot of the address have been scribbled through and pages are loose. I have learned. I brought them stickers with me this time. I've got some stickers that goes up on the left-hand side with your return address. Then, I've got to put stamps on them. Just a whole melee or whatever you might call it. And it's a hell of a mess. I did a real good job, at least I thought so. There was one that I didn't have to send off, and that was for my daddy. So, I kept it separate, so I thought.

I got it all tended to and dashed over to the post office, put them in the slot and thought it was all done. I went to bed that night about eleven o'clock and it hit me all of a sudden—I sent Daddy's card in the mail. I didn't have address on it. I was going to hand deliver it. It didn't have nothing on it but "Daddy," no stamp, so I knew that it wouldn't get to Daddy. I said, "Holy Moly!" Fifty dollars just shot in the wind.

I got back in my truck and was coming to town. I was looking in my address book, and believe it or not, I had stuck it in my address book. So I don't have to do anything. I was going to go to the post office to see if they had it, but this worked out good.

I finished this thing up and me and my wife, like to go to restaurants. She couldn't stand me having them free gift cards for $20. She had to go yesterday to spend that. Of course, naturally, I've got to put some more with it. We weren't really hungry. It was at dinner. We got us a hamburger and she got a salad and, of course, that run $35, so I had to put $15 with the twenty. She gave them the gift card and we put the money in that little book, you know how they do it, where you have to leave the money in the book.

I left in one direction and my wife went the other in her car. About the time she got in the car, somebody knocked on the window. It was that girl that waited on us. My wife said that she acted like she was scared to death. She said, those gift cards didn't go into effect until next week, and I reckon she was going to have to pay that $20 out of her pocket.

I asked my wife, "What if you didn't have $20?"

Well, I don't know what they'd have done. Maybe she didn't mention it to the manager. Maybe it just upset her, but if she had mentioned it to the manager, maybe he would not have made her pay. If he did, he would have been a piss-poor manager. I could have handled that. All he had to do was put $20 out of miscellaneous in there and just earmark them gift cards until they were due the next day. I don't know. It'll all work out.

Speaking of restaurant, that gift card thing ain't just what you think it is. We had to wait until the proper date to use them things. I don't even like that restaurant, but we had the cards, so we went back and was going to use them $20 worth of gift cards. Come to find out, you can't use but five dollars at the time. In other words, I've got to go to the restaurant four times to get my $20 back. I think I am just going to give them the $15.

Johnny

I worked on a job one time, building a house with a man, and I came to know as Johnny. I began to watch him—I never saw him doing anything—but when a truck would come with materials, he would sign for it. Later on, I found out he was foremen of the job. I befriended him. Found out that he worked for the man that owned all the property, hundreds of acres etc., and he was in charge of getting everything done from bottom to top. The owner didn't even live here. He had a lot of responsibility. He was a short guy and wore a big hat. Lots of little man wear big hats and will drive big trucks. He told me what he made and I could not believe it.

Later on, I went by another job site and he had quit. I was thinking how in the world you quit that kind of a job making good money. Before he went to work for this man, he worked on the road for the state but it was contract work. He worked for himself. Evidently, he liked that better.

I happened to run in to him later on, and he had started a small business and was just getting started. He called me to work in his house. He had five hundred acres with virgin timber and it was off the highway down a three-path road. Probably a mile. He was getting married, and he had built himself a shack close to the woods with a chainsaw. I mean, he built the whole house with the chainsaw. You could tell it—one bed room, little bath and a kitchen. He said that he was getting married so he guessed he needed to add on a bigger bed room because she had a son and he had son. He said that he might ought to put in a septic tank. I told him I'd work for him but it will be a little while.

I went back to see him a little later at his business, and he had a young man there with him about seven or eight years old. He introduced him to me as his new son. The little boy was very well mannered and I kind of liked him. His hair came down on his neck like some of these kids do now. Johnny said, "Dumbo, you see that long hair? He won't have it tomorrow. Nobody that works for me has long hair and he won't either." Next day, his hair was cut.

Now, he had gotten married before I came back, and they got married in his office. He sold three buildings during the ceremony. Three buildings in middle of ceremony! When is the last time you heard of that?

After they got married, she went back to her hometown. She was a school teacher. They never even went to lunch, let alone a honeymoon. Her son went home with him. He said that his son will stay with him a couple of weeks and learn the rules and then she was coming. He was workaholic. He had his food on the table at the restaurant at 5 o'clock a.m. every morning. He allows himself 10 to 15 minutes to eat and he was gone.

The next morning, they went in at 5 o'clock as usual. He called the restaurant and ordered something for his son to eat. Johnny ate his breakfast and said to the little boy, "Let's go to work."

The little boy said, "Dad, I have not eaten my breakfast yet."

Johnny said, "That's all right. You will eat in the morning." They left and he put him to work, helping him put up fence post.

The son said, "Dad, the gnats are eating me up."

He said, "Son, do you know what you do about that?"

"No, dad."

"You just eat the gnats."

The woman that used to clean Johnny's house said that she would never stay out there. It was isolated. Ran into him 10 or 15 years later, first thing I asked him, "You still married?"

He said, "Yeah, I am Dumbo. I have got a mansion out there beside my shack, and the boys are getting grown. By the way, let me tell you what I did this weekend. We had a road check."

I said, "What is a road check?"

He said, "Dumbo it was a full moon and you could see nearly as good as day time. I parked my truck in the middle of my three-path road and left my lights on. About 11 o'clock, her 16 year old son came cutting down through there. He stopped and said, 'What is it Dad?' Road check, son. I had him blow in my hat then I drew a line in the sand with my cane and told him to 'walk this line'. The boy walked the line. But son, I can tell you have been drinking some but I drank some when I was young and you are not drunk but you are an hour late, so you are grounded for a week."

The boy said, "Yes, dad." The boy went on home.

A few minutes later, his 18 year old son came cutting down through there, and he did the same thing with him. He walked the line and blow in the hat. He told his son the same thing that he was grounded for one week. The boy said, "Yes, dad."

He had a piece of cardboard on the wall with ten things to do such as, take out the trash, sweep the floor, make up your bed etc. I guess they both went by the rules.

Both the boys wound up graduating from college and had good jobs and married and come to see their mama and daddy often. I some time wonder if tough love is not the best way. He bought his son a big new truck with all the trimmings at 16 years old. Early on he got a DUI. Dad let him spend the night in jail. Next morning, he went with him to the Ford place. He asked the salesman if they had a good old truck. They did and he bought it and sold the new one, and told his son that would be the way he traveled until he graduated.

Viagra

One of my acquaintances went to a doctor for a checkup. The doctor asked him, "How is your sex life?"

The man said, "What sex life?"

The doctor gave him a bottle of pills and told him to take four pills, thirty minutes before sex. Saturday afternoon he decided it was time, and all of a sudden, he remembered he had something to do in town. So, he ran to the bathroom, took the four pills before going to town and believed this will work out just right. He figured that he won't be gone too long. He started in town. It hit him! He may have taken Ambien by mistake. He dashed back home and checked—he had taken the wrong one. He tried to regurgitate to no avail, but he went on back to town. He knew the people he had to see will be gone before long so he had to go on. He had to get there first. He had a small business that paid on Saturdays if he caught them. If not, they would blow it over weekend.

He left there and went to the health clinic, he told them what he had done and they said, "You are still standing up?"

He said, "Yes I am fine."

"Go to the emergency room now."

He vaguely remembers driving up under the shelter. The next thing he knew, he woke up, and he was freezing, and alarms started going off and the lights came on and the nurse came in. They had him on suicide watch. All he had on was that half shirt that they furnish you. He said that he had wires running all over him. He asked the nurse, "Where the hell am I?"

She said, "Sir, you are in the hospital."

Then, it hit him what he had done. He said, "I am getting the hell out of here." He got off the bed.

She said, "Sir you can't leave."

He said, "The hell I can't."

"Sir, if you leave, the insurance won't pay." So, he sat down the bed. He thought to himself *what the hell do I do now.*

All his buddies had found out about it, plus everyone in town. He was ashamed of himself, and everybody laughed at him. They called his wife and told her. It was so funny. He said that he would like to kick them in the ass. But when he finally got home his wife was not mad at all.

Chicken Gizzards

We went out dancing one night and wind up at a woman's house. One of the constituents got up in middle of the night and ate the woman's chicken gizzards. Next morning, she got up and said, "Where's all my chicken gizzards?"

He said, "I am sorry. I ate them all, and they were really good."

She said, "I was just thawing them out. I had not cooked them yet."

Smittie

We were playing poker at an all-night poker game at a man's house. He charged so much per hour, this guy name Smittie, when he won a pot, he would say, "You monkey's sure are tough." He would laugh get up and go to the bathroom, and would be back before the next hand was dealt. I tell you, that is fast pissing.

One night, the owner followed him to the bathroom. On the way to the bathroom, he ate his poodle's dog food, and pissed in the carpet all the way to the commode and all the way back to the poker table. The owner ran his ass off.

Septic Tank

A woman was having trouble with her septic tank—they lived in the country. She said that she don't know what could be wrong. They were very careful about what they flush down the commode. I noticed there were three young girls sitting on the porch. The woman came and watched us dig the septic tank lid up. There were condoms floating all over the water. She said, "Girls!" We looked and the girls were gone. I wonder why?

Cousin's Money

I had a cousin who had a furniture store. He had sold his accounts to a loan agency, and he had the cash money. He was going to a bigger town and buy more furniture. He got drunk that night, and went to the small restaurant about day light. He flirted with a waitress and told her about the money he had. She decided to quit her job and go with him.

They wound up bogged down on a beach. The law caught them and took them to jail. While there, the law counted his money and wanted to know where he got it. Therefore, she knew how much he had, and that he cancelled buying the furniture and started home.

They got about halfway to a little town with motels. She really wanted to have sex, so they stayed the night. Next morning, they got up and he took her home. He went home and went to bed. That afternoon, he decided to check his money. If you ever played poker or been to a real good party, you kind of know that you peep in your bill fold because you would know how much money you have. He peeped in the bill fold and figured he had plenty.

Next morning, he went to work and checked again and the hundred-dollar bills had changed to one-dollar bills. He went to her house, knocked on her door, screaming and raising the hell. Her brother was there, and he was a bad ass crook. He had killed a man. He opened the door and pointed a pistol right between his eyes and told him if he did not leave right then, he would kill him. That was the end of that. He was short about four thousand dollars.

Canadian

This fellow took a job out of town and did not have anywhere to stay. A man from Canada offers him to stay with him for a week or so. He told me that night, after dinner, that man and his wife and sister and him sat down to watch movies of the man catching fish in Canada. His sister was a knockout and was about 23 years old. All of the sudden, the movie changed to pornography and that was first time he had ever seen it. He said that he noticed that this man's wife started smooching and his sister was smiling at him. In a little while, the man said that he and his wife were going to bed to make love. He let him know that his sister had broken up with her boyfriend from Canada. That man told him to take her and make love to her in her bedroom.

He said, "Okay."

He was really looking forward to it. He said, "There were no chairs, so I sat down on edge of the bed with her."

She had an 8 x 10 envelope with a picture of her boyfriend. She wanted to show him, and it was his private parts. They stretched more than ten inches from one side to the other. He said that it took his breath away. He told her that her boyfriend was nice looking, got up and went to his bed. He never tried to bother her again. He was too afraid that it would be too embarrassing for him.

Giffords

There was a place five or ten miles from town that the young man went after they got rid of their dates Saturday night. All it was, was a little shack with a juke box in it and a beer cooler. A lot of us went, and we would stand outside laugh drink and have a good time. It was open 24/7.

One night some of my friends got mad with the owner. They got their guns and shot the juke box out and all the windows etc. It scared them. The young men were afraid of going to jail. It was tobacco cropping time in Canada and they hauled ass to Canada.

Two of them have been staying with me. They went by the cleaners and got my heavy jackets and some more of my clothes before they left. After a while, most of them came home but there were two that I know of that wound up in California. They would call me occasionally. One of them married and worked there. The other one went to work with a big chain company as a flunkies. I read in the paper a while back, and he had retired as one of the top executives. He even owned several of their franchises in different states and he had just died.

Flippers

We were going fishing in my big boat on the coast. I decided I need some more tires. I hooked it up and started to town. But I did not have it locked down. There were two ponds you had to cross in between. In other words, a pond on both sides of the road. There was a big dip there that served as a spillway. I was going too fast, I looked back and my boat was passing me. It came off the ball of my truck when I hit the dip. It was airborne. But, luckily it landed in the pond.

I say that because if it had not, the asphalt on the road would have broken it bad. It went between the trees and was floating away. I did not know what to do, so I went home and got my little boat and was going to try somehow to get it out of the pond. Oh, by the way, it was sinking, the plug was out.

Luckily, my young neighbor was home and went back with me. The boat and the boat trailer were nose to nose and the chain was holding them together. I had a car buckle and the other guy could not loosen it. We had a pair of pliers and dived in and loosened it. He put the plug in boat, and I drove it to shore. I thought that the trailer would sink, but I guess the air in the tires must have keep it off the bottom. Because we pulled it all the way out and it did not hit any of the stumps that I knew were there.

By that time, there were a lot of drug store cowboys and they told me they had already called 911 flipper people to come and rescue the truck and see if anybody had drowned. I said, "You did what?"

"Called 911."

I said, "Call those people back. That's my boat and my truck did not sink."

We live in a small town and could just see the news media out taking pictures of me and my truck, boat and trailer. Everyone that knew me would say, 'well, Dumbo has done it again.'

Friend in Hospital

I had an older associate that was wealthy. I really liked him and we had some things in common like real estate etc. I told him about an interest rate at a bank, and he deposited a good bit of money there. They sent me a check for getting his business. My other associates could not stand that.

He was in the hospital in ICU and I went to see him. I asked the nurse which room Mr. Bent was in and I went to the room. I recognized him, he was tall, slender, old, and he had a breathing mask on. There was a lady in there with him. I presumed to be his wife. We talked a few minutes, and I told her the story about the bank giving me the money for getting him as a customer. She questioned me, seemed surprised. I told her again and she said, "How much did he put in there?"

It hit me something was wrong. I asked her what his name was. It was James Bent. My friend's name was Elvin Bent. In other words, I was in the wrong damn room. The lady at the desk should have told me there were two Bents in there. I made a fool of myself.

Sneakie His Way

Sneakie had been living with one of his drinking buddies and I think they fell out. He gave Sneakie forty dollars and took him to city limits and dropped him out. Sneakie said that he had to take his belt off and put it around his suitcase to keep it closed, and had to hold his pants up on the other hand. He did not know where he was going or what he was going to do when he got there.

He wound up in another town with a menial job and someone told him about a woman who had recently widowed that was very well fixed. He knew she would be with friends on Saturday night. He got a haircut, a new leisure suit, new shoes, walked in the door, spotted her and asked her to dance. WHAM BAM BOOGAL BANG. She fell for him like a ton of rocks. They married before long.

He continued to be Sneakie, but with lots more money. He had a good time, but she loved him. So, he got by with it. She died first and when he died all he had left was a little house he probably owed for. Sneakie liked to borrow money. I think it made him feel important. He said that if he had to live his life over, he would not change a damn thing. He said that he did it his way. I wish we were going fishing in the morning.

In the end, I stayed with my small business and have done better than I deserve. I still have problems once in a while but I have a wonderful wife. That helps. And I still have a golf cart and another puppy dog and

Sammie L. O'Steen

I am recording again. If people like this book and I live long enough I might write another. I have thoroughly enjoyed it and wish I wasn't through. It has been like serenity for me. I feel as though I have gotten rid of some things that have been bottled up in me for 40 to 50 years. I have plenty of stories left.

Printed in the USA
CPSIA information can be obtained
at www.ICGtesting.com
LVHW021416240524
780937LV00015B/1030